# CHILDREN'S
## ATLAS

### EIGHTH EDITION

## David and Jill Wright

# CONTENTS

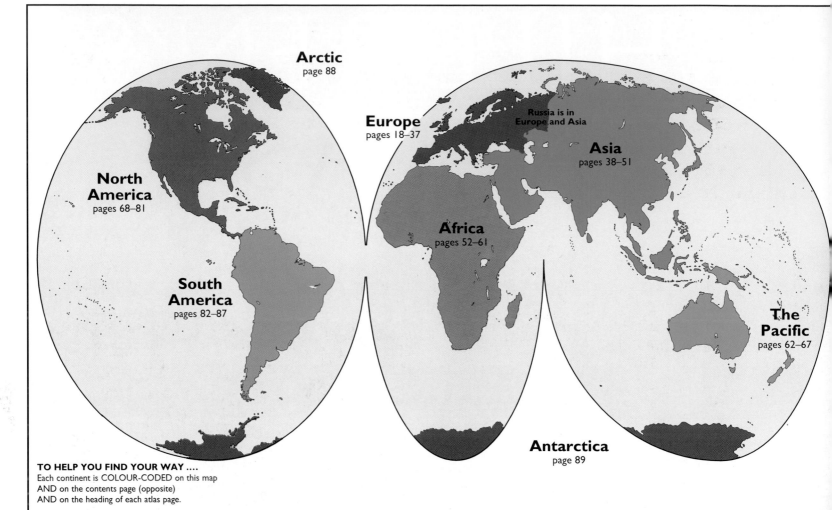

Arctic
page 88

Europe
pages 18–37

Russia is in
Europe and Asia

Asia
pages 38–51

North
America
pages 68–81

Africa
pages 52–61

South
America
pages 82–87

The
Pacific
pages 62–67

Antarctica
page 89

**TO HELP YOU FIND YOUR WAY ....**
Each continent is COLOUR-CODED on this map
AND on the contents page (opposite)
AND on the heading of each atlas page.

**TO RACHEL AND STEVEN**

**EXECUTIVE EDITOR** Caroline Rayner

**ART EDITORS** Alison Myer, Karen Ferguson

**EDITOR** Kara Turner

**PICTURE RESEARCH** Liz Fowler

**COVER PHOTO ACKNOWLEDGEMENTS**

**FRONT COVER:**
**Colorsport** /Bryan Yablonsky top left
**Michel Gunther/Still Pictures** centre top left
**Robert Harding Picture Library** /Christopher Rennie
top right
**Image Bank** /Harald Sund bottom left
**Tony Stone Images** bottom right, /Stephen Beer
centre bottom right, /Tim Davis centre top right
**David & Jill Wright** centre bottom left

**BACK COVER:**
**Panos Pictures** /Gary John Norman bottom left
**Tony Stone Images** /Walter Geierserger top right

First published in Great Britain in 1987
by George Philip Limited,
a division of Octopus Publishing Group Limited,
Michelin House, 81 Fulham Road, London SW3 6RB

**Eighth and fully revised edition 1997**
Reprinted 1998

Text © 1987, 1997 David and Jill Wright
Maps © 1998 Octopus Publishing Group Ltd

Cartography by Philip's

A CIP catalogue record for this book is available from the British Library.

ISBN 0–540–07239–7

Printed in Hong Kong

# OUR PLANET EARTH

O ur Earth is made of layers of rock. The diagram below shows the Earth with a slice cut out. The hottest part is the core, at the centre. Around the core is the mantle.

The outer layer, the crust, is quite thin under the oceans, but it is thicker under the continents. Scientists now know that the Earth's crust is cracked, like the shell of a hard-boiled egg that has been dropped. The cracks are called faults. The huge sections of crust divided by the faults are called plates and they are moving very, very slowly. The continents have gradually moved across the Earth's surface as the crustal plates have moved. Sudden movements near the faults cause volcanic eruptions or earthquakes.

*The Earth from space:* this satellite image shows Africa, Arabia and Antarctica. The Sahara Desert is free of cloud and all sunny. Some of the white clouds near the Equator show thunderstorms. In the far south, the Antarctic ice is even whiter than the cloud.

Can you name the oceans to the west (left) and to the east (right) of Africa? The map on page 7 will help you.

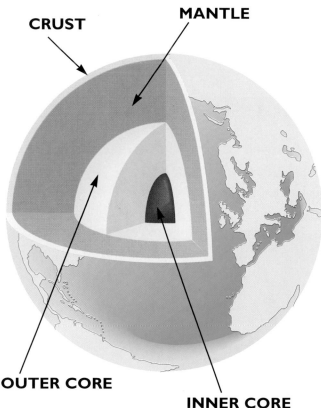

**CRUST**

**MANTLE**

**OUTER CORE**

**INNER CORE**

## FACTS ABOUT THE EARTH

**DISTANCE AROUND THE EQUATOR** 40,075 kilometres
**DISTANCE AROUND THE POLES** 40,007 kilometres
**DISTANCE TO THE CENTRE OF THE EARTH** 6370 kilometres
**SURFACE AREA OF THE EARTH** 510,065,600 square kilometres
**PROPORTIONS OF SEA AND LAND** 71% sea; 29% land
**DISTANCE FROM THE EARTH TO THE SUN** 150,000,000 kilometres
  (It takes 8½ minutes for the Sun's light to reach the Earth.)
**DISTANCE FROM THE EARTH TO THE MOON** 384,400 kilometres
**THE EARTH TRAVELS AROUND THE SUN** at 107,000 kilometres per hour,
  or nearly 30 kilometres per second
**THE EARTH'S ATMOSPHERE** is about 175 kilometres high
**CHIEF GASES IN THE ATMOSPHERE** Nitrogen 78%; oxygen 21%
**AVERAGE DEPTH OF SEA** 3900 metres
**AVERAGE HEIGHT OF LAND** 880 metres

It takes 365¼ days for the Earth to travel all the way round the Sun, which we call a year. Every four years we add an extra day to February to use up the ¼ days. This is called a Leap Year. The Earth travels at a speed of over 107,000 kilometres an hour. (You have travelled 600 kilometres through space while reading this!)

As the Earth travels through space, it is also spinning round and round. It spins round once in 24 hours, which we call a day. Places on the Equator are spinning at 1660 kilometres an hour. Because of the way the Earth moves, we experience day and night, and different seasons during a year (see page 13). No part of our planet is too hot or too cold for life to survive.

Our nearest neighbour in space is the Moon, 384,400 kilometres away. The first men to reach the Moon took four days to travel there in 1969. On the way, they took photos of the Earth, such as the one on the left. The Earth looks very blue from space because of all the sea. It is the only planet in the Solar System with sea. Look at the swirls of cloud, especially to the south of Africa. These show that the Earth has an atmosphere. Our atmosphere contains oxygen and water vapour, and it keeps all living things alive. The diagrams below show all the planets of our Solar System.

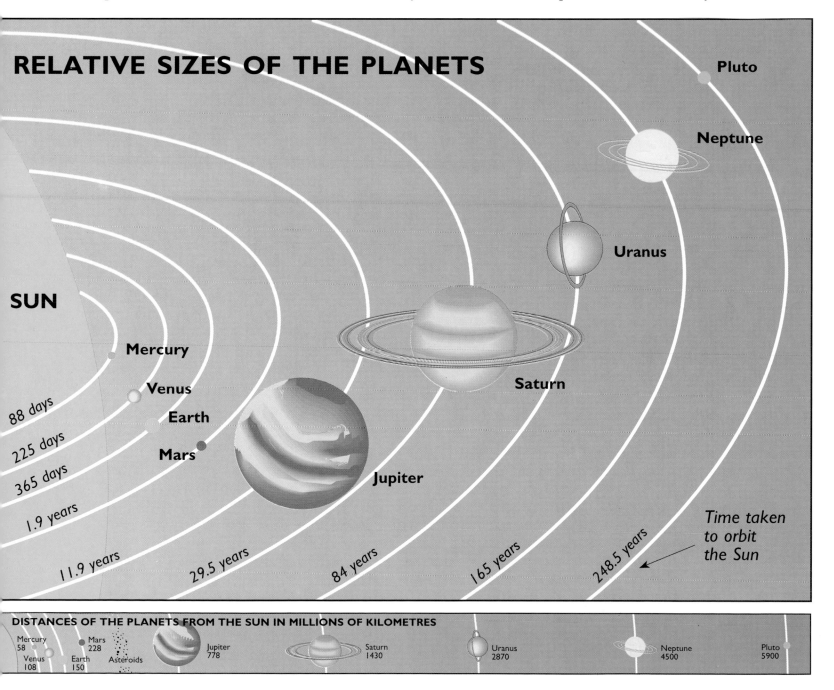

## RELATIVE SIZES OF THE PLANETS

Pluto

Neptune

Uranus

SUN

Mercury

Venus

Saturn

Earth

88 days

Mars

225 days

365 days

Jupiter

1.9 years

11.9 years

29.5 years

84 years

165 years

248.5 years

*Time taken to orbit the Sun*

**DISTANCES OF THE PLANETS FROM THE SUN IN MILLIONS OF KILOMETRES**

| Mercury 58 | Mars 228 | Asteroids | Jupiter 778 | Saturn 1430 | Uranus 2870 | Neptune 4500 | Pluto 5900 |
| Venus 108 | Earth 150 | | | | | | |

# MOUNTAINS, PLAINS AND SEAS

*Mountains and plains – but in which country? (Answer on page 96.)*

**T**he map shows that there is much more sea than land in the world. The Pacific is by far the biggest ocean; the map splits it in two.

The mountains are shown with shadows on this map. Look for the world's highest mountain range – the Himalayas, in Asia. There are high mountains on the western side of both American continents. Most of the world's great mountain ranges have been made by folding in the Earth's crust.

Desert areas are shown in orange. The green expanse across northern Europe and northern Asia is the world's biggest plain.

**Farming the Great Plains of North America.** *The Plains cover large areas of the USA and Canada. This land in Alberta, Canada, has just been harvested. The almost flat land of the Great Plains ends where the Rocky Mountains begin.*

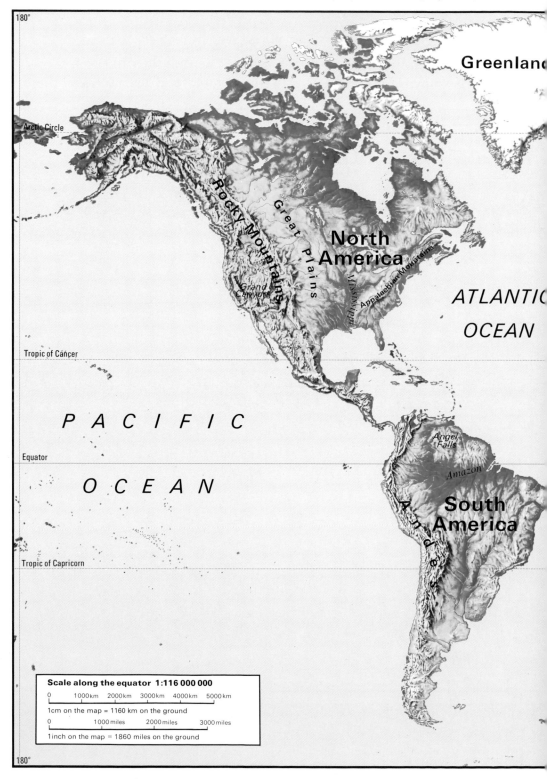

180°

Greenland

Arctic Circle

Rocky Mountains

Great Plains

North America

Mississippi

Appalachian Mountains

Grand Canyon

ATLANTIC OCEAN

Tropic of Cancer

PACIFIC

OCEAN

Equator

Angel Falls

Amazon

South America

Andes

Tropic of Capricorn

180°

**Scale along the equator  1:116 000 000**

0    1000km   2000km   3000km   4000km   5000km

1cm on the map = 1160 km on the ground

0           1000 miles        2000 miles       3000 miles

1inch on the map = 1860 miles on the ground

## WORLD RECORDS: LARGEST · LONGEST · HIGHEST · DEEPEST

**LARGEST OCEAN** Pacific, 179,679,000 sq km
**DEEPEST PART OF OCEANS**
  Mariana Trench, 11,022 metres (Pacific)
**LARGEST LAKE** Caspian Sea, 360,700 sq km
  (Europe and Asia)
**DEEPEST LAKE** Lake Baykal, 1940 metres
  (Russia)

**LONGEST RIVERS** Nile, 6670 km (Africa);
  Amazon, 6448 km (South America);
  Yangtze, 6380 km (Asia)
**LARGEST ISLANDS** Australia, 7,686,848
  sq km; Greenland, 2,175,600 sq km
**LARGEST DESERT** Sahara, 8,400,000 sq km
  (Africa)

**HIGHEST MOUNTAIN** Everest, 8848 m (Asia)
**LONGEST MOUNTAIN RANGE** Andes,
  7200 km (South America)
**LONGEST GORGE** Grand Canyon, 349 km
  (North America)
**HIGHEST WATERFALL** Angel Falls,
  979 metres (Venezuela, South America)

COPYRIGHT. GEORGE PHILIP & SON. LTD.

# THE COUNTRIES OF THE WORLD

*The United Nations flag* – but what do the symbols mean? (Answers on page 96.)

**F**ive of the continents of the world are divided into countries. Most countries are now independent and manage their own affairs. A few of the smaller countries and islands are still ruled by another country.

Look at the boundaries between countries. Some follow natural features, such as rivers or mountain ranges. Straight boundaries were drawn for simplicity. But in many places they separate people of the same language or tribe, and this can create problems.

Remember – no world map on flat paper can show both the size *and* the shape of a country correctly – only a globe is really accurate.

*The United Nations building,* in New York City, USA. The world's problems are discussed here – and sometimes solved. Almost every country has a representative at the United Nations.

Greenland

RUSSIA

Alaska (U.S.A.)

CANADA

UNITED STATES OF AMERICA (U.S.A.)

Bermuda

Tropic of Cancer

Hawaiian Islands

MEXICO

BAHAMAS

CUBA

JAMAICA

DOMINICAN REPUBLIC

BELIZE

HONDURAS

HAITI

PUERTO RICO

GUATEMALA

EL SALVADOR

NICARAGUA

TRINIDAD & TOBAGO

COSTA RICA

PANAMA

VENEZUELA

GUYANA

SURINAM

French Guiana

COLOMBIA

Equator

ECUADOR

BRAZIL

PERU

BOLIVIA

Tropic of Capricorn

FRENCH POLYNESIA

PARAGUAY

CHILE

URUGUAY

ARGENTINA

Falkland Islands

South Georgia

**KEY**

| | |
|---|---|
| ARM. = ARMENIA | LUX. = LUXEMBOURG |
| AZER. = AZERBAIJAN | MAC. = MACEDONIA |
| B. = BHUTAN | MOL. = MOLDOVA |
| B.-H. = BOSNIA-HERZEGOVINA | N. = NETHERLANDS |
| BUR. = BURUNDI | R. = RWANDA |
| BEL. = BELGIUM | SL. = SLOVENIA |
| CRO. = CROATIA | S. = SWITZERLAND |
| L. = LEBANON | U.A.E. = UNITED ARAB EMIRATES |
| LITH. = LITHUANIA | YUGO. = YUGOSLAVIA |

**Scale along the equator  1:116 000 000**

0    1000km  2000km  3000km  4000km  5000km

1cm on the map = 1160 km on the ground

0         1000miles      2000 miles      3000 miles

1inch on the map = 1860 miles on the ground

## WHICH ARE THE WORLD'S BIGGEST COUNTRIES?

Only five of the 'top ten' countries with large populations are also among the 'top ten' biggest countries.

### TOP TEN COUNTRIES BY SIZE (SQUARE KILOMETRES)

| | | | | | |
|---|---|---|---|---|---|
| 1 | Russia | 17,075,000 | 6 | Australia | 7,686,850 |
| 2 | Canada | 9,976,140 | 7 | India | 3,287,590 |
| 3 | China | 9,596,960 | 8 | Argentina | 2,776,890 |
| 4 | USA | 9,372,610 | 9 | Kazakstan | 2,717,300 |
| 5 | Brazil | 8,511,970 | 10 | Sudan | 2,505,810 |

### TOP TEN COUNTRIES BY POPULATION (UN FIGURES)

| | | | | | |
|---|---|---|---|---|---|
| 1 | China | 1227 million | 6 | Russia | 148 million |
| 2 | India | 943 million | 7 | Pakistan | 144 million |
| 3 | USA | 264 million | 8 | Japan | 125 million |
| 4 | Indonesia | 199 million | 9 | Bangladesh | 118 million |
| 5 | Brazil | 161 million | 10 | Mexico | 93 million |

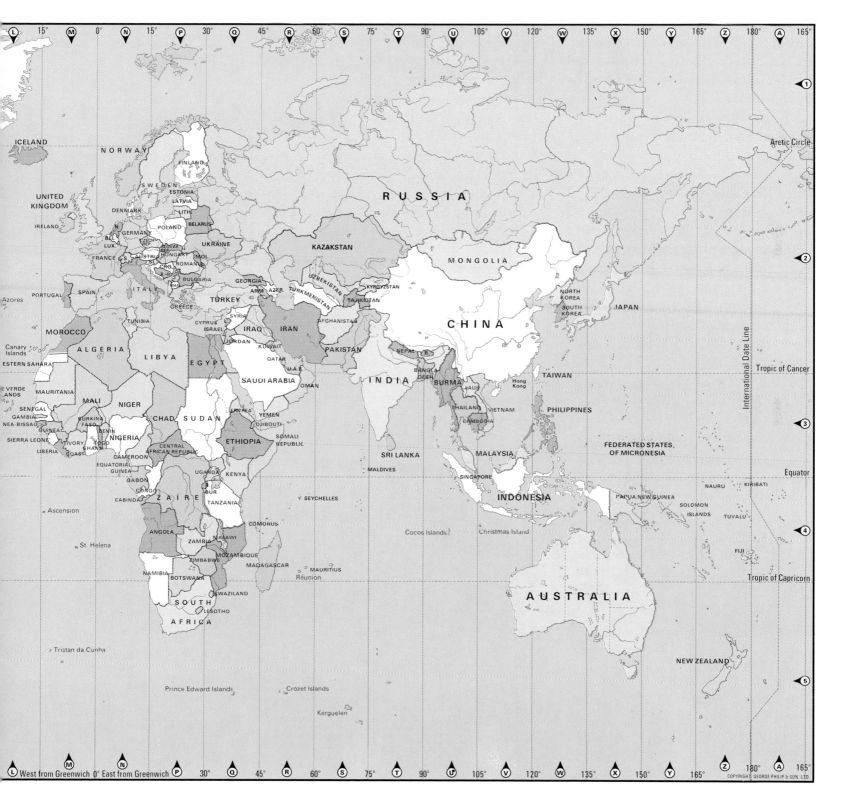

# PEOPLE OF THE WORLD

**T**here is *one* race of people: the human race. In Latin, we are all known as *Homo sapiens* – 'wise person'. The differences between people, such as dark or light skin, hair and eyes, are small.

The smaller map (below) shows the rich and the poor countries of the world. In any one country there are rich and poor people, but the difference between countries is even greater.

The map shows that the richest countries are in North America, north-west Europe, parts of the Middle East, Japan and Australia. Here, most people usually have enough to eat. They can buy a variety of different foods; they can go to a doctor when they need to, and the children can go to school.

The poorest countries (shown in dark green) are in the tropics – especially in Africa and southern Asia. Life in these countries is very different from life in the rich world. Many people struggle to grow enough food, and they are often hungry. People who do not have enough to eat find it difficult to work hard and they get ill more easily. They do not have enough money to pay for medicines or to send their children to school to learn to read and write. Some of the poorest people live in shanty towns in or near large cities.

But many people in the tropics do manage to break out of this 'cycle of poverty'. They now have a better diet, and more and more people can obtain clean water. Primary schools now teach most children to read and write and do simple arithmetic – though there are few books and classes may be very large. In many places, village health workers are taught to recognize and treat the common diseases.

**Crowded and poor: a shanty town in Brazil.** *These shanties on a steep hillside in Rio de Janeiro were built by people who have nowhere else to live. Some of them have low-paid jobs, but others have to beg to get enough to eat.*

## THIRD WORLD AID

Watering onions in The Gambia, West Africa. This boy's watering-can was given by a charity to help the family grow more food. The onions can be sold to people living in the city. Many schemes like this are helped by money given by the rich countries of the world.

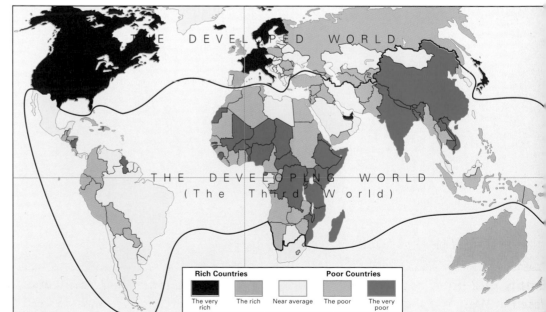

THE DEVELOPED WORLD

THE DEVELOPING WORLD
(The Third World)

| Rich Countries | | | Poor Countries | |
|---|---|---|---|---|
| The very rich | The rich | Near average | The poor | The very poor |

The map on this page shows where the world's people live. Most of the world has very few people: large areas are shown in yellow.

These areas are mostly desert, or high mountains, or densely forested, or very cold. Over half the world's people live in the lowlands of south and east Asia. Other crowded areas are parts of north-west Europe and the Nile Valley. The most crowded places of all are the big cities.

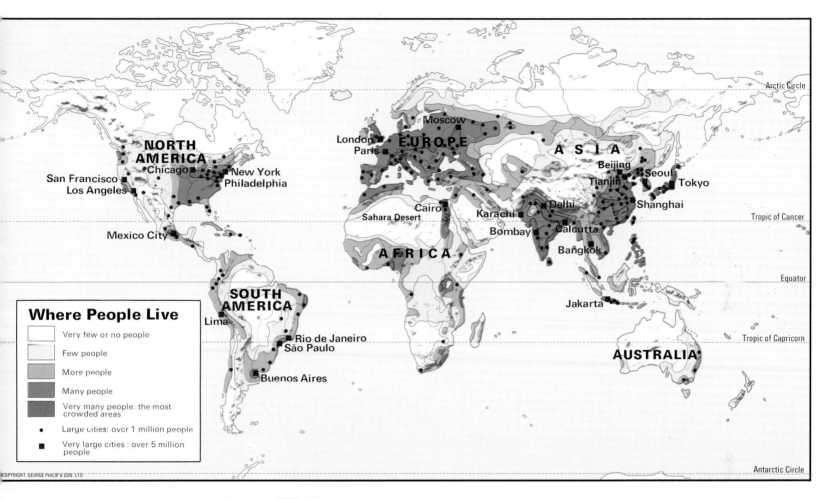

**Where People Live**

| | |
|---|---|
| | Very few or no people |
| | Few people |
| | More people |
| | Many people |
| | Very many people: the most crowded areas |
| • | Large cities: over 1 million people |
| ■ | Very large cities : over 5 million people |

**Empty and poor:** nomads meet in the desert in Western Sahara. It is hot and dusty and there is no shade.

**Crowded and rich: New York City.** The offices of Manhattan Island, in the centre of New York, are crowded with workers during the day, but are empty at night. Only the richest people can afford to live in apartments here.

# COLD AND HOT LANDS

**F**ive important lines are drawn across these maps of the world: the Arctic and Antarctic Circles; the Tropics of Cancer and Capricorn; and the Equator. They divide the world roughly into *polar*, *temperate* and *tropical* zones.

The *polar* lands remain cold all through the year, even though the summer days are long and some snow melts.

The *temperate* lands have four seasons: summer and winter, with spring and autumn in between. But these seasons come at different times of the year north and south of the Equator, so children in New Zealand open their Christmas presents in midsummer.

The *tropical* lands are always hot, except where mountains or plateaus reach high above sea level. For some of the year the sun is directly overhead at noon (local time).

The map on THIS page shows the world in June. Hardly anywhere is very cold (except for Antarctica in midwinter, of course). Most of the very hot areas in June are NORTH of the Equator.

The December map (opposite page) is very different. Both Canada

**Arctic winter.** *Winter begins early in Greenland. This fishing boat is frozen in the harbour at Angmagssalik, near the Arctic Circle. There are 24 hours of dark and cold at Christmas. Yet by June, the ice will have melted, and there will be 24 hours of daylight.*

and Russia are VERY cold. Most of the hottest areas in December are SOUTH of the Equator, near the Tropic of Capricorn.

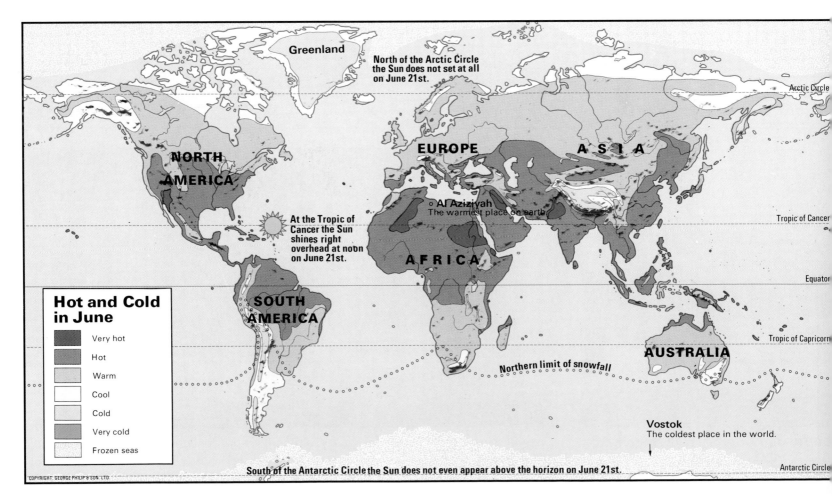

Greenland

North of the Arctic Circle the Sun does not set at all on June 21st.

Arctic Circle

NORTH AMERICA

EUROPE

ASIA

At the Tropic of Cancer the Sun shines right overhead at noon on June 21st.

o Al Aziziyah
The warmest place on earth

Tropic of Cancer

AFRICA

Equator

SOUTH AMERICA

**Hot and Cold in June**

- Very hot
- Hot
- Warm
- Cool
- Cold
- Very cold
- Frozen seas

Northern limit of snowfall

AUSTRALIA

Tropic of Capricorn

**Vostok**
The coldest place in the world.

South of the Antarctic Circle the Sun does not even appear above the horizon on June 21st.

Antarctic Circle

COPYRIGHT: GEORGE PHILIP & SON LTD.

## COLD & HOT LANDS FACTS

**HOTTEST RECORDED TEMPERATURE**
58°C at Al Aziziyah in Libya

**COLDEST RECORDED TEMPERATURE**
−89.2°C at Vostok in Antarctica

**GREATEST CHANGE OF TEMPERATURE AT ONE PLACE IN A YEAR**
From −70°C to +36.7°C at Verkhoyansk in Siberia, Russia

**HIGHEST RAINFALL IN ONE MONTH**
9299 mm in one month at Cherrapunji, India *

**HIGHEST RAINFALL IN ONE YEAR**
26,461 mm in one year at Cherrapunji *

**MOST RAINY DAYS**
350 days in a year at Mount Wai-'ale-'ale in Hawaii *

**WETTEST PLACE ON AVERAGE**
Over 11 metres of rain a year at Tutunendo, Colombia *

**DRIEST PLACE** In the Atacama Desert, northern Chile: no rain for 400 years! *

**MOST THUNDER** 322 days in a year with thunder at Bogor in Java, Indonesia

* See map on page 14.

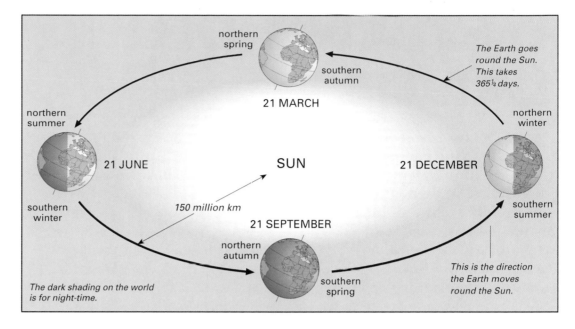

The Earth goes round the Sun. This takes 365¼ days.

northern spring / southern autumn — 21 MARCH

northern summer / southern winter — 21 JUNE — SUN — 150 million km

21 DECEMBER — northern winter / southern summer

21 SEPTEMBER — northern autumn / southern spring

This is the direction the Earth moves round the Sun.

The dark shading on the world is for night-time.

The seasons are different north and south of the Equator. In June it is summer in North America, Europe and Asia. The sun is overhead at the Tropic of Cancer. The North Pole is tilted towards the sun, and the Arctic enjoys 24 hours of daylight. Notice that Antarctica is in total darkness.

By December, the Earth has travelled half way round the sun. The sun is overhead at the Tropic of Capricorn. Antarctica now has 24 hours of daylight.

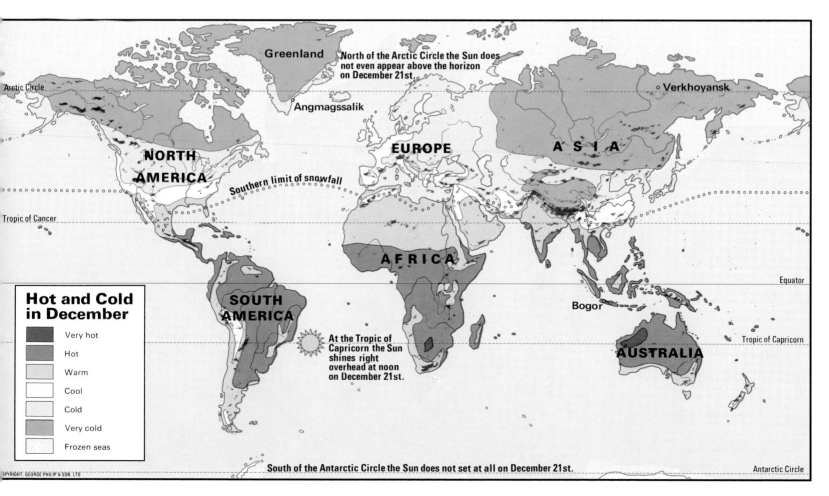

Greenland — North of the Arctic Circle the Sun does not even appear above the horizon on December 21st

Arctic Circle

Verkhoyansk

Angmagssalik

NORTH AMERICA

EUROPE

ASIA

Southern limit of snowfall

Tropic of Cancer

AFRICA

SOUTH AMERICA

Bogor

Equator

At the Tropic of Capricorn the Sun shines right overhead at noon on December 21st.

Tropic of Capricorn

AUSTRALIA

**Hot and Cold in December**

- Very hot
- Hot
- Warm
- Cool
- Cold
- Very cold
- Frozen seas

South of the Antarctic Circle the Sun does not set at all on December 21st.

Antarctic Circle

COPYRIGHT GEORGE PHILIP & SON LTD

# WET AND DRY LANDS

**W**ater is needed by all living things. The map below shows that different parts of the world receive different amounts of water. Follow the line of the Equator on the map: most places near the Equator are very wet as well as being very hot.

The map on the opposite page shows that near the Equator there are large areas of thick forest. Here, it rains almost every day. Now follow the Tropic of Cancer and the Tropic of Capricorn on both maps. The Tropics cross areas of desert, where it is dry all year.

Between the desert and the forest is an area of tall grass and bushes called the savanna. People here talk about the 'wet' and 'dry' seasons. For part of the year it is as rainy as at the Equator; for the rest of the year it is as dry as the desert.

North of the Sahara Desert is the Mediterranean Sea. Places around this sea have lovely hot, dry summers, but they do have rain in winter. There are areas near other deserts with a similar climate, such as California in North America and central Chile in South America, and around the Cape of Good Hope in the far south of Africa.

**Forest and mountains in Alberta, Canada.** *The coniferous trees can survive Canada's bitterly cold winters. In the high mountains, trees cannot grow it is too cold and the soil is too thin.*

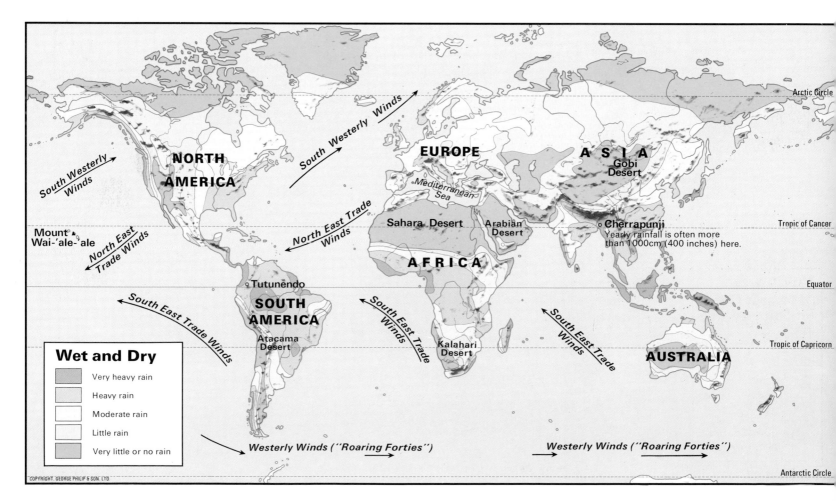

**Wet and Dry**

- Very heavy rain
- Heavy rain
- Moderate rain
- Little rain
- Very little or no rain

COPYRIGHT. GEORGE PHILIP & SON. LTD.

14

In the temperate lands, many places have some rain all through the year. Damp winds from the sea bring plenty of rain to the coastal areas, and trees grow well. Far inland, near the centre of the continents, and where high mountains cut off the sea winds, it is much drier. Here, there are vast grasslands, like the prairies of North America and the steppes of Russia. In the centre of Asia, there is a desert with very cold winters.

Temperate forests stretch right across North America, Europe and Asia – except where they have been cleared for farmland and towns.

In the far north there is 'tundra' which is snow-covered for many months in winter, and marshy in the short summer.

Finally, Greenland and Antarctica are mostly snow and ice.

*Burning the savanna, in northern Ghana, West Africa. At the end of the long dry season, farmers burn the bush (long grass and small trees). The land will be ready for planting crops when it rains.*

*Sand dunes in the desert in Namibia, southern Africa. The Namib Desert has given its name to the country of Namibia. It is a very dry area, west of the Kalahari Desert.*

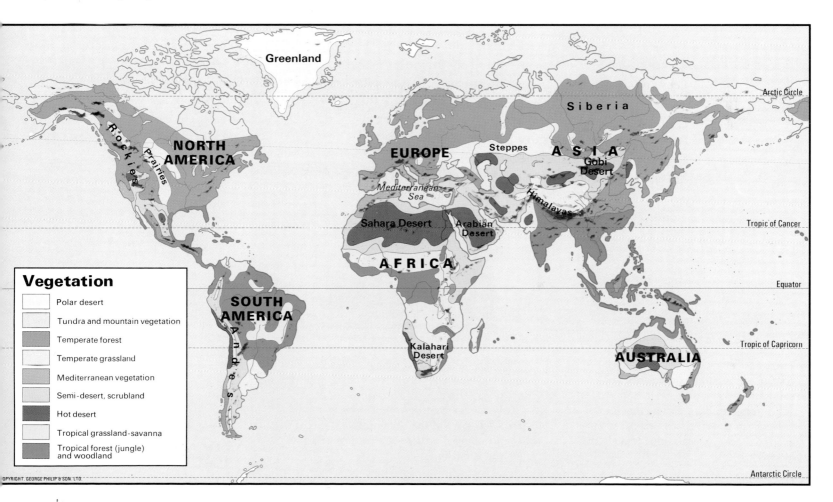

**Vegetation**

| | |
|---|---|
| | Polar desert |
| | Tundra and mountain vegetation |
| | Temperate forest |
| | Temperate grassland |
| | Mediterranean vegetation |
| | Semi-desert, scrubland |
| | Hot desert |
| | Tropical grassland-savanna |
| | Tropical forest (jungle) and woodland |

**15**

# ENJOYING MAPS

The world is round, so the best possible model is a globe. It is impossible to draw a really accurate map of the round world on a flat piece of paper. The world maps on pages 6 to 9 and 11 to 15 have the right shape for the land, but the size of northern lands is too big. The map on page 10 has the wrong shapes but the size is right: it is an 'equal-area' map.

The area maps (pages 18 to 89) show the continents and countries of the world. Each map has a key, with information that will help you to 'read' the map. Use your imagination to 'see' what the land is like in each part of the world that you visit through these pages. The photos and text will make your picture clearer.

These two pages explain the key to all the maps. The country of Ghana is used as an example. Ghana is in square B2 of the map (right). Find ⓑ at the top of the map with one finger, and ②➤ at the side of the map with another finger. Move each finger in the direction of the arrows; Ghana is where they meet.

The capital city of each country is underlined on the maps. The rulers of the country live in the capital city, and it is the biggest city in most countries. But not all capital cities are big. On this map, you can see three sizes of city. The biggest ones are marked by a square; they have over one million people. Middle-sized cities have a big circle, and smaller cities have a small circle. Small towns and villages are not shown on maps of this scale, but some have been included in this atlas because they are mentioned in the text.

**The border between Ghana and Burkina Faso.** *The red lines on the map show the boundaries between countries. When travelling from one country to another, you have to stop at the border. These children live in Ghana and their flag flies on their side of the border.*

*'BYE-BYE SAFE JOURNEY' is the message on the arch. In Ghana, most officials speak English. In Burkina Faso officials speak French.*

## POSTAGE STAMPS ... are on many pages of this atlas

You can learn so much from stamps! The map shows you that Ghana is a country; the stamps tell you the official language of Ghana, and show you Ghana's flag.

The map tells you that Ghana has a coastline; the 10Np stamp tells you the name of Ghana's main port, and shows you the big modern cranes there.

The map shows that this port is very near to Accra, which is the capital city of Ghana.

The map tells you the name of Ghana's biggest lake (man-made). The 6Np stamp shows you the dam and its name.

You can see that they chose the narrowest part of the valley to build the dam. On page 57, there is a picture of a ferry on the lake.

## COINS OF THE WORLD

The Ghana coin (left) shows cocoa pods growing on the branches of a cocoa tree. Cocoa is a major export from Ghana. Another Ghana coin (right) shows traditional drums.

Other countries also picture familiar items on their coins. **Nigeria** has a palm tree on its coins; **The Gambia** has a sailing ship on one of its coins (see page 53).

But don't believe everything you find on coins: there is a LION on the 10p UK coin!

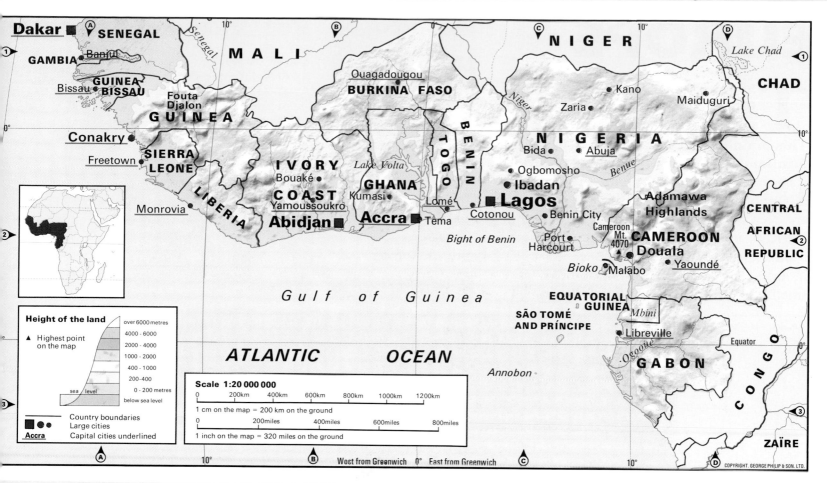

Scale 1:20 000 000
0 200km 400km 600km 800km 1000km 1200km
1 cm on the map = 200 km on the ground
0 200miles 400miles 600miles 800miles
1 inch on the map = 320 miles on the ground

COPYRIGHT. GEORGE PHILIP & SON. LTD.

West from Greenwich 0° East from Greenwich

## HEIGHT OF THE LAND

The countries of West Africa
are coloured so that you can
tell the height of the land.
Green shows the lowest
land. Often the real land will
not look green – in the dry
season the grass is brown. The higher land is
coloured brown, even though some parts are
covered with thick green forest! The highest
point in West Africa is shown with a small black
triangle – find it in square C2 – but the mountains
are not high enough to be shown in mauve or white:
look for these on page 45. And to find land below
sea level, try page 25. In West Africa, Cameroon has
some dramatic mountains, but elsewhere the change
from lowland to highland is often quite gentle.
The 'shadows' on the map help you to see which
mountains have steep slopes.

Water features – the ocean, big rivers and lakes –
are in blue, and their names are in *italic print*.

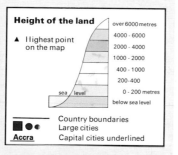

Height of the land
▲ Highest point on the map
over 6000 metres
4000 - 6000
2000 - 4000
1000 - 2000
400 - 1000
200-400
sea level
0 - 200 metres
below sea level

■ ● • Country boundaries
Large cities
**Accra** Capital cities underlined

## SCALE

This box
shows the
scale of the map. The scale can be written in different
ways. The map is drawn to a scale of 1:20,000,000,
which means that the distance between two places
on the ground is exactly 20 million times bigger than
it is on this page! Other maps in this atlas are drawn
to different scales: little Belgium (page 25) is drawn
at a scale of 1:2 million, while the largest country in
the world is drawn at a scale of 1:45 million (Russia,
page 41). Another way of writing the scale of this
map is to say that 1 centimetre on the map is equal
to 200 kilometres on the ground in West Africa.

You can use the scale line to make your own scale
ruler. Put the straight edge of a strip of paper against
the scale line and mark the position of 0, 200, 400,
600 kilometres, etc. Carefully number each mark.
Now move your scale ruler over the map to see
how far it is between places. For example, Accra
to Abidjan is 400 kilometres.

Scale 1:20 000 000
0 200km 400km 600km 800km 1000km 1200km
1 cm on the map = 200 km on the ground
0 200miles 400miles 600miles 800miles
1 inch on the map = 320 miles on the ground

# EUROPE

**T**he map shows the great North European Plain that stretches from the Atlantic Ocean to Russia. This plain has most of Europe's best farmland, and many of the biggest cities.

To the north of the plain are the snowy mountains of Scandinavia. To the south are even higher mountains: the Pyrenees, the Alps and Carpathians, and the Caucasus Mountains. Southern Europe has hills and mountains by the Mediterranean Sea. The small areas of lowland are carefully farmed.

## EUROPE FACTS

**AREA** 10,531,000 sq km (including European Russia). Europe is the smallest continent.
**HIGHEST POINT** Mt Elbrus (Russia), 5633 metres
**LOWEST POINT** By Caspian Sea, minus 38 metres
**LONGEST RIVER** Volga (Russia), 3690 km
**LARGEST LAKE** Caspian Sea*, 360,700 sq km
**BIGGEST COUNTRY** Russia*, 17,075,000 sq km (total area – Europe and Asia)
**BIGGEST ALL-EUROPEAN COUNTRY** Ukraine, 603,700 sq km
**SMALLEST COUNTRY** Vatican City* (in Rome, Italy), less than half a square kilometre!
**MOST CROWDED COUNTRY** Malta
**LEAST CROWDED COUNTRY** Iceland
* A world record as well as a European record

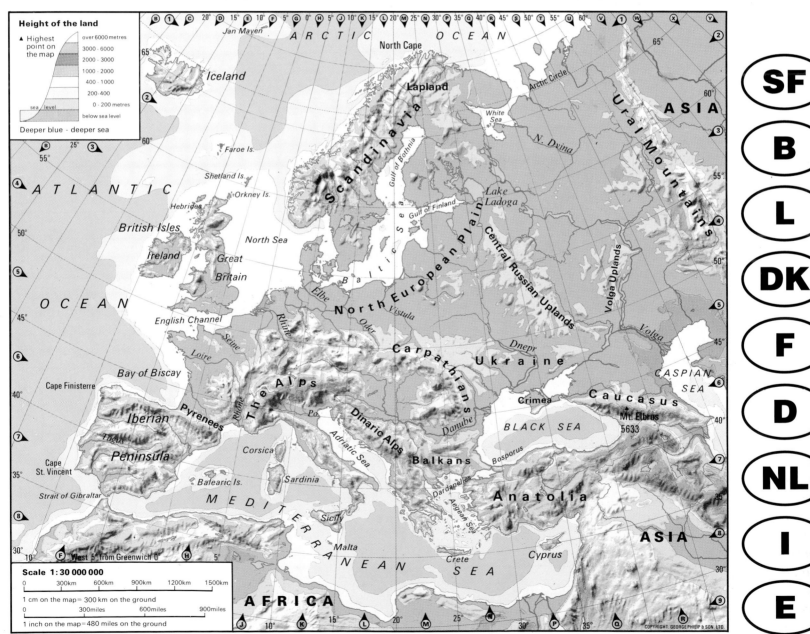

**Northern Europe: Iceland.** *Lake okulsarlon has many small icebergs which break off the glacier that comes from the ice-cap. Ice melts to make the lake.*

**Central Europe: Austria.** *The Dachstein Mountains are part of the Alps. They are high enough to have patches of snow even in summer. The valley floors are farmed.*

**Southern Europe: Sardinia.** *The island of Sardinia is part of Italy and is in the Mediterranean. It is very hot and dry in the summer. It is a popular holiday destination.*

S
IRL
A
GB
P
GR

*hese 15 ar-plates are rom the 15 ountries of he European Union. Can ou name hem? Answers on age 96.)*

The countries of Georgia, Armenia and Azerbaijan are really in Asia but are also included on this map and on page 37 because they are at a larger scale.

# SCANDINAVIA

**AREA** 338,130 sq km
**POPULATION** 5,125,000
**MONEY** Markka

### DENMARK

**AREA** 43,070 sq km
**POPULATION** 5,229,000
**MONEY** Krone

The five countries that make up Scandinavia are rich and successful, yet the people live further north than in almost any other part of the world.

The total population of each of these countries is small, and very few people live in the far north. Most people live in towns and cities, with excellent central heating in their houses and flats.

Farming is difficult this far north because the winters are long and cold. Scandinavia has hardly any minerals except for iron ore in Sweden and oil under the North Sea. The mountains of Norway make travel difficult, but there are good train and boat services.

**Geiranger fjord, Norway,** is one of many long, narrow inlets of the sea along the Norwegian coast. Glaciers dug these deep, steep valleys. The village is on the flat land at the head of the fjord. The steep mountains mean that the best way to travel is often by boat.

## LEGOLAND MODEL VILLAGE

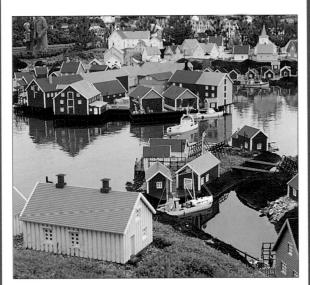

Legoland is a model village beside the Lego factory in Denmark. Everything in the village is made of Lego! There are models of famous buildings as well as ordinary houses from different parts of the world. The photograph shows the model of a typical fishing village in the Lofoten Islands, which are off the northern coast of Norway. The Lego man and his friends can be found in shops all over the world!

**Lake Saimaa, Finland,** is one of hundreds of lakes in the southern part of that country. Only the largest are shown on the map. During the Ice Age, ice-sheets scraped hollows in the rock which filled with water after the ice melted.

**AREA** 323,900 sq km
**POPULATION** 4,361,000
**MONEY** Krone

### SWEDEN

**AREA** 449,960 sq km
**POPULATION** 8,893,000
**MONEY** Swedish krona

**Reindeer in Lapland.** Lapland is the northern part of Norway, Sweden and Finland, where the Lapps live. They keep reindeer for their milk, meat and leather, and also to pull sledges. Notice the warm and colourful clothes the Lapps wear. In winter, it is dark here even at midday, but in summer it is light at midnight.

The mountains of Iceland and Norway are high and rugged. There are large ice-sheets and glaciers even today.

Denmark and southern Sweden are low-lying. The soil is formed from sand, gravel and clay brought by ice-sheets in the Ice Age.

***Stockholm harbour, Sweden:*** *this fine nineteenth-century sailing ship is now a Youth Hostel for visitors to the Swedish capital. Stockholm is built on lots of islands around a large harbour. It is fun to explore the city by boat.*

## LAND OF ICE AND FIRE

**Iceland has many volcanoes.** *Most are quiet and peaceful (above left). But... sometimes a great volcanic eruption lights up the night sky and the light is reflected in the sea (above right).*

*Only 260,000 people live in Iceland. It is near the Arctic Circle and there is ice on the mountains, in glaciers and ice-sheets. A warm Atlantic current keeps the sea ice-free and it is full of fish. Iceland has an important fishing fleet.*

ARCTIC OCEAN

ICELAND
Vatnajökull
Akureyri
Reykjavík
Keflavik
Surtsey

Vesterålen
Lofoten Islands

North Cape
Vardö
Kirkenes
L. Inari
Tana
Tromsö
Lapland
Narvik
Muonio
Torne
Kiruna
Bodö
Kemi
Lule
Kemi
Luleå
Oulu
L. Oulu

Arctic Circle

NORWAY
SWEDEN
RUSSIA
FINLAND

Trondheim
Ålesund
Storsjön
Östersund
Vaasa
Kuopio
Galdhöpiggen 2469
Jotunheimen
Sundsvall
Glåma
Sogne Fjord
Lillehammer
Mjösa L.
Bergen
Hardanger Fjord
Sörfjord
Oslo
Gävle
Gulf of Bothnia
Tampere
L. Saimaa
Vänern
Örebro
Västerås
Uppsala
Åland Is.
Turku
Helsinki
Kristiansand
Stockholm
Gulf of Finland
L. Vätter
Norrköping
ESTONIA
Skagerrak
Skagen
Jönköping
Gotland
Gothenburg
Öland
Baltic Sea
Aalborg
Kattegat
DENMARK
Jutland
Aarhus
Sjælland
Copenhagen
Esbjerg
Odense
Malmö
Bornholm
GERMANY
POLAND

**Scale 1:10 000 000**
0      100km    200km    300km    400km
1 cm on the map = 100 km on the ground
0          100miles          200miles
1 inch on the map = 160 miles on the ground

**Height of the land**
▲ Highest point on the map
over 6000 metres
4000 - 6000
2000 - 4000
1000 - 2000
400 - 1000
200 - 400
sea level   0 - 200 metres
below sea level

■ ● • Country boundaries
Large cities
**Oslo** Capital cities underlined

EUROPA CEPT
ÍSLAND 85

JARDELDAR Á HEIMAEY 1973
ÍSLAND 25

# THE UK AND IRELAND

## UK

**AREA** 243,368 sq km
**POPULATION** 58,306,000
**MONEY** Pound sterling
**CAPITAL** London
**FLAG** Union Jack

*Ireland:* Long ago, horses were used for ploughing the fields – a skilled job. But today, 'horse-power' means petrol and machines.

The United Kingdom is made up of Great Britain (England, Wales and Scotland) and Northern Ireland. The UK was the most important country in the world 150 years ago. Many old factories and coal mines have now closed down, and several million people have no jobs.

Much of the UK is still quiet and beautiful, with very varied scenery. The north and west of Great Britain are made of old, hard rocks. This area is higher and wetter than the south and east, and has pasture for cattle and sheep. Most of the arable farming is in the lower, drier and flatter south and east.

**Bodiam Castle** is in the county of Sussex, south of London. It was built over 600 years ago against a possible French invasion. Today it is a ruin surrounded by a fine moat and its 'invaders' are tourists. The tourist industry is very important for the UK, and visitors come from all over the world to visit historic places.

## IRELAND

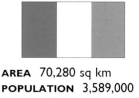

**AREA** 70,280 sq km
**POPULATION** 3,589,000
**MONEY** Irish pound
**CAPITAL** Dublin

**Rugby football** was invented last century by a schoolboy at an English private school at Rugby. It is very popular in Wales – the hosts of the Rugby World Cup competition in 1999.

## STAMP

Can you spot 8 famous London landmarks on this stamp?
(Answers on page 96.)

**Dublin, capital of the Republic of Ireland,** is built beside the River Liffey. These fine old houses overlooking the river are now carefully preserved. A quarter of the country's population lives in Dublin and its suburbs.

**The Somerset Levels,** south of Bristol in south-west England. The foreground was marshland which has been drained – it is below the level of high tides.

**The Republic of Ireland** is a completely separate country from the UK. There were twice as many people in Ireland 150 years ago as there are today. Farming is still important, but new factories have been built in many towns. Even so, many Irish people have moved to the UK or to the USA to find work.

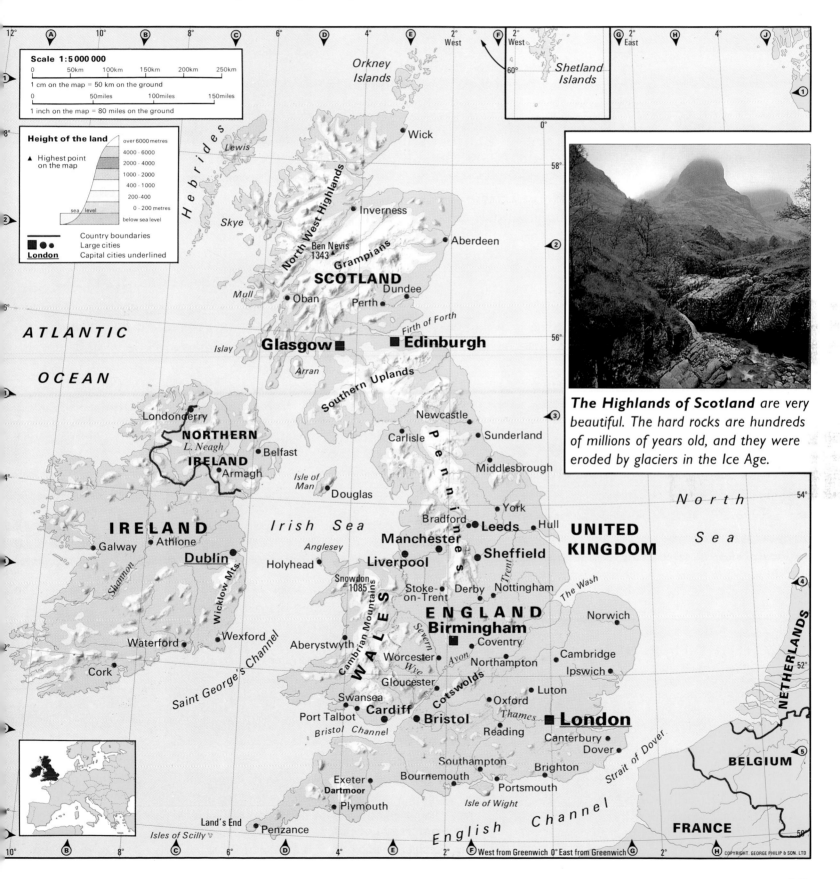

Scale 1:5 000 000

0  50km  100km  150km  200km  250km

1 cm on the map = 50 km on the ground

0  50miles  100miles  150miles

1 inch on the map = 80 miles on the ground

**Height of the land**

▲ Highest point on the map

over 6000 metres
4000 - 6000
2000 - 4000
1000 - 2000
400 - 1000
200 - 400
0 - 200 metres
below sea level

sea level

Country boundaries
Large cities
**London** Capital cities underlined

*ATLANTIC*

*OCEAN*

*Hebrides*

*Lewis*

*Skye*

*Mull*

*Islay*

*Arran*

*Orkney Islands*

Wick

*North West Highlands*

Inverness

Aberdeen

Ben Nevis 1343 ▲

*Grampians*

**SCOTLAND**

Oban

Dundee

Perth

*Firth of Forth*

**Glasgow** ■  ■ **Edinburgh**

*Southern Uplands*

Newcastle

Carlisle

Sunderland

Middlesbrough

*Shetland Islands*

60°

58°

56°

*North*

*Sea*

54°

Londonderry

**NORTHERN**

*L. Neagh*

Belfast

**IRELAND**

Armagh

*Isle of Man*

Douglas

**IRELAND**

Galway

Athlone

**Dublin**

*Irish Sea*

*Anglesey*

Holyhead

York

Hull

*Pennines*

Bradford

**Leeds**

**Manchester**

**Liverpool**

**Sheffield**

**UNITED**

**KINGDOM**

*Shannon*

Snowdon 1085

Stoke-on-Trent

Derby

Nottingham

*Trent*

*The Wash*

Waterford

Wexford

*Saint George's Channel*

*Cambrian Mountains*

**W A L E S**

**E N G L A N D**

Birmingham

Coventry

Norwich

Cambridge

Ipswich

Cork

Aberystwyth

Worcester

*Severn*

*Avon*

Northampton

*Wye*

Gloucester

*Cotswolds*

Luton

Oxford

Swansea

**Cardiff**

Port Talbot

**Bristol**

*Thames*

■ **London**

Reading

Canterbury

Dover

*Bristol Channel*

Southampton

Brighton

*Strait of Dover*

Exeter

**Dartmoor**

Bournemouth

Portsmouth

*Isle of Wight*

Plymouth

Land's End

Penzance

*Isles of Scilly*

*English Channel*

**NETHERLANDS**

52°

**BELGIUM**

**FRANCE**

50°

*Wicklow Mts.*

**The Highlands of Scotland** *are very beautiful. The hard rocks are hundreds of millions of years old, and they were eroded by glaciers in the Ice Age.*

12°  10°  8°  6°  4°  2° West  2° West  2° East  4°

0°

10°  8°  6°  4°  2° West from Greenwich 0° East from Greenwich 2°

COPYRIGHT. GEORGE PHILIP & SON. LTD

**23**

# BENELUX

## NETHERLANDS

AREA 41,526 sq km
POPULATION 15,495,000
MONEY Guilder

## BELGIUM

AREA 30,510 sq km
POPULATION 10,140,000
MONEY Belgian franc

**B**enelux is a word made up from BElgium, NEtherlands and LUXembourg. Fortunately, the first two letters of each name are the same in most languages, so everyone can understand the word. These three countries agreed to co-operate soon after World War 2. But they still have their very own King (of Belgium), Queen (of the Netherlands), and Grand Duke (of Luxembourg).

The Benelux countries are all small and are the most crowded in mainland Europe, but there is plenty of countryside too. Most of the land is low and flat, so they are sometimes called the Low Countries.

## LUXEMBOURG

AREA 2,590 sq km
POPULATION 408,000
MONEY Luxembourg franc

*Are these windmills?* Most Dutch 'windmills' are really wind-pumps. They were used to pump water up from the fields into rivers and canals. The river is higher than the land! These are at Kinderdijk, east of Rotterdam.

## GAINING LAND

The map shows that a large part of the Netherlands is below sea level. For over 1000 years, the Dutch have built dykes (embankments) to keep out the sea and rivers. Then the water is pumped out. Once they used wind-pumps; today they use diesel or electric pumps. The rich farmland grows vegetables and flowers.

*Bruges* is a historic town in Belgium. These old houses have survived many wars. Canals run through the town. The houses have no back door or garden – but they get a lovely view!

## SPOT THE DIFFERENCE

What is the difference between these two coins from Belgium? And why is there a difference? (Answers on page 96.)

*Europort, Rotterdam.* Rotterdam is by far the biggest port in the whole world. Ships come from all over the world, and barges travel along the River Rhine and the canals of Europe to reach the port. Whole families live on the barges; sometimes they even take their car with them!

## PUZZLE

*A puzzle from the Netherlands:*
● What are these yellow objects?
● What are they made of?
● Why are they for sale? (Answers on page 96.)

Luxembourg and eastern Belgium have pleasant wooded hills called the Ardennes. Once, there was a flourishing steel industry using coal from Belgium and iron ore from Luxembourg. Today, most of the coal mines have closed and central Belgium is a problem area.

The eastern part of the Netherlands has large areas of heath and forest. But the best-known landscape is the 'polders' of the west.

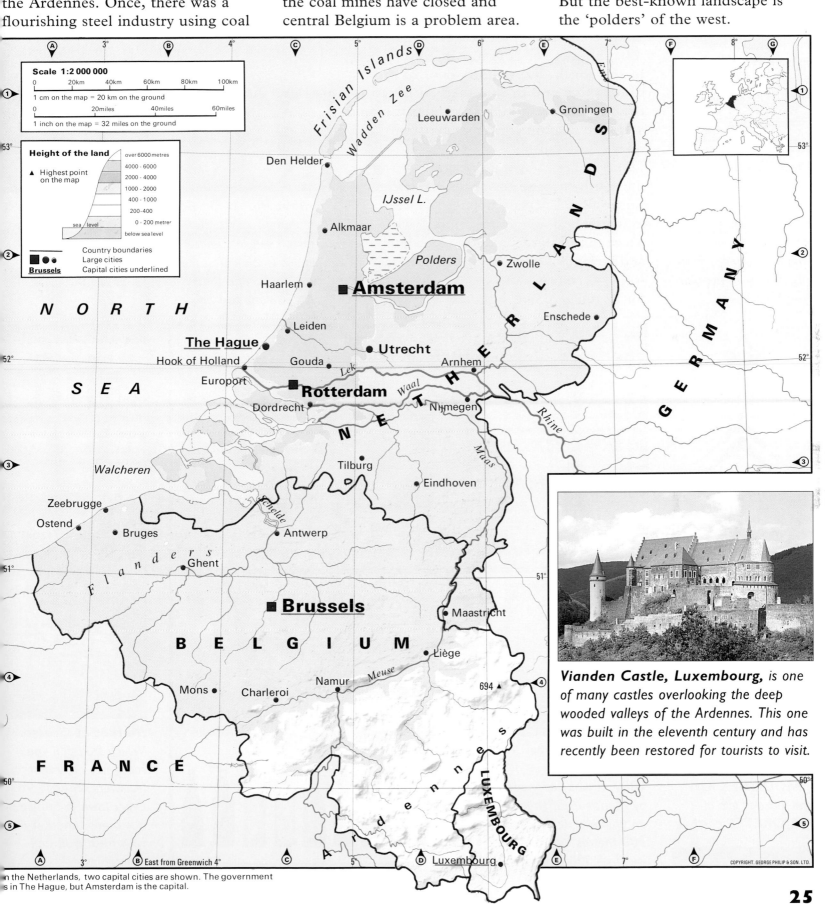

**Scale 1:2 000 000**

| 0 | 20km | 40km | 60km | 80km | 100km |

1 cm on the map = 20 km on the ground

| 0 | 20miles | 40miles | 60miles |

1 inch on the map = 32 miles on the ground

**Height of the land**

▲ Highest point on the map

over 6000 metres
4000 - 6000
2000 - 4000
1000 - 2000
400 - 1000
200 - 400
0 - 200 metrer
below sea level

sea level

Country boundaries
Large cities
**Brussels** Capital cities underlined

Frisian Islands
Wadden Zee
Leeuwarden
Groningen
Den Helder
IJssel L.
Alkmaar
Polders
Zwolle
Haarlem
■ **Amsterdam**
N E T H E R L A N D S
Enschede
Leiden
**The Hague**
**Utrecht**
Hook of Holland
Gouda
Lek
Arnhem
Europort
Waal
■ Rotterdam
Dordrecht
Nijmegen
Rhine
NORTH
SEA
Walcheren
Maas
Tilburg
Eindhoven
Zeebrugge
Scheldt
Ostend
Bruges
Antwerp
Flanders
Ghent
Maastricht
■ **Brussels**
Liège
B E L G I U M
Namur
Meuse
Mons
Charleroi
694 ▲
F R A N C E
Ardennes
LUXEMBOURG
Luxembourg
GERMANY

East from Greenwich 4°

COPYRIGHT. GEORGE PHILIP & SON. LTD.

**Vianden Castle, Luxembourg,** *is one of many castles overlooking the deep wooded valleys of the Ardennes. This one was built in the eleventh century and has recently been restored for tourists to visit.*

n the Netherlands, two capital cities are shown. The government s in The Hague, but Amsterdam is the capital.

# FRANCE

*These Majorette models are made in France. They include a Renault van, a Michelin lorry, an Air France bus and a Paris bus. The most popular French cars are:*

France is a country with three coastlines: can you see which these are? It is hot in summer in the south, but usually cool in the mountains and in the north. France is the biggest country in Western Europe, so there are big contrasts between north and south.

The highest mountains are the Alps in the south-east and the Pyrenees in the south-west. They are popular for skiing in winter and for summer holidays too. More than half the country is lowland, and farming is very important. Besides fruit, vegetables and wine, France is famous for its many different cheeses and wines.

**Mont Blanc.** *The 'White Mountain' is the highest mountain in Western Europe. It is 4807 metres high. Even in summer (as here) it is covered in snow. Cable-cars take tourists and skiers up the mountain, and there is a road tunnel through Mont Blanc to Italy.*

**RENAULT**

**CITROËN**

**PEUGEOT**

*What else can you find in your home that is made in France? In our home we have: **BIC** ball-point pens, **LE CREUSET** frying-pans and saucepans, **ARCOROC** glassware, **ARCOPOL** cups, a **MOULINEX** mixer, and lots and lots of **MAJORETTE** cars!*

**The Eiffel Tower** *was built in Paris in 1889. It was designed by Monsieur Eiffel, an engineer. It is 300 metres high and weighs 7000 tonnes!*

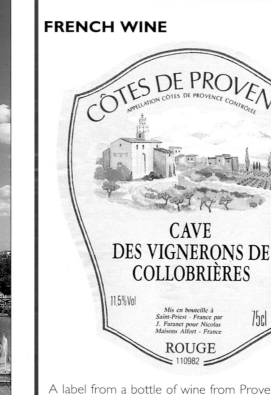

**FRENCH WINE**

CÔTES DE PROVENCE
APPELLATION CÔTES DE PROVENCE CONTRÔLÉE

CAVE
DES VIGNERONS DE
COLLOBRIÈRES

11,5%Vol

Mis en bouteille à
Saint-Priest - France par
J. Faranet pour Nicolas
Maisons Alfort - France

75cl

ROUGE
110982

A label from a bottle of wine from Provence, in the south of France. It shows a village in Provence, with fruit trees and long, straight rows of vines.

**AREA** 551,500 sq km
**POPULATION** 58,286,000
**MONEY** Franc

**Market at Grasse.** *Which fruit can you recognize on this stall? (Answers on page 96.) Every town in France has a good market with fresh fruit and vegetables.*

France is changing fast. The number of people living in villages is going down, and the population of the cities is growing – partly swelled by Arabs from North Africa who have come to live in France. The biggest city is Paris, which is also the capital. Ten million people live in the Paris region, and five big new towns have been built around Paris. 'Disneyland Paris' brings many more tourists to the area.

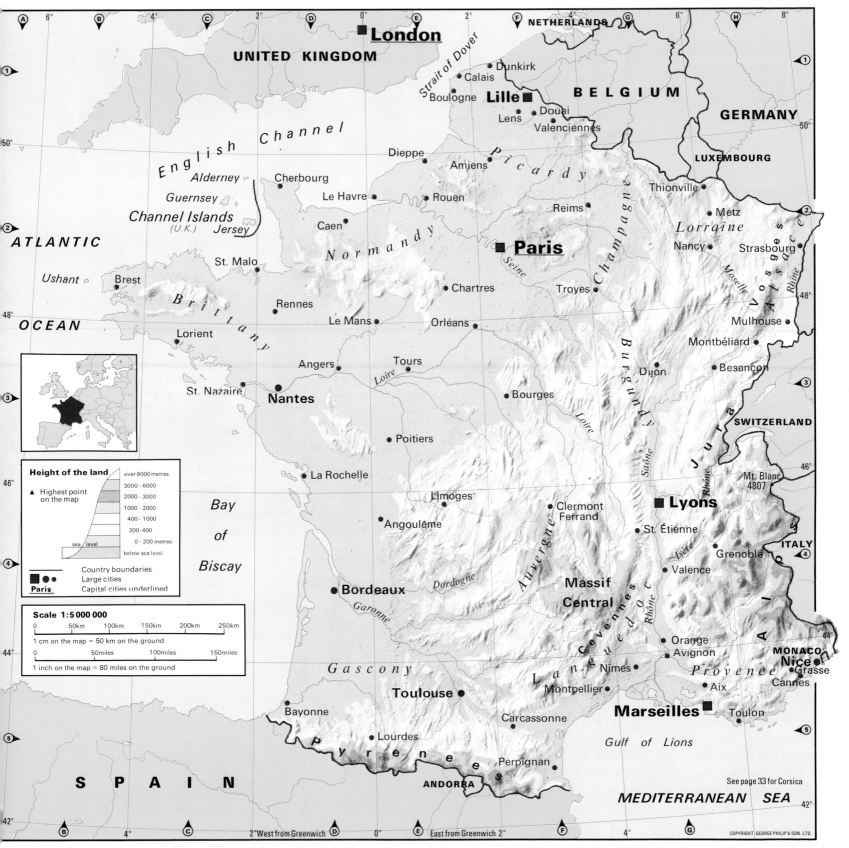

Height of the land

over 6000 metres
3000 - 6000
2000 - 3000
1000 - 2000
400 - 1000
200 - 400
0 - 200 metres
below sea level

▲ Highest point on the map

sea level

■ ● ● Country boundaries
Large cities
**Paris** Capital cities underlined

Scale 1:5 000 000

0   50km   100km   150km   200km   250km

1 cm on the map = 50 km on the ground

0   50miles   100miles   150miles

1 inch on the map = 80 miles on the ground

NETHERLANDS
London
UNITED KINGDOM
Dunkirk
Calais
Boulogne
Lille
BELGIUM
Lens
Douai
Valenciennes
GERMANY
Strait of Dover
English Channel
Dieppe
Amiens
Picardy
LUXEMBOURG
Thionville
Metz
Alderney
Cherbourg
Le Havre
Rouen
Reims
Lorraine
Guernsey
Channel Islands
(U.K.) Jersey
Caen
Normandy
Paris
Seine
Troyes
Champagne
Nancy
Strasbourg
ATLANTIC
St. Malo
Chartres
Vosges
Alsace
Moselle
Rhine
Ushant
Brest
Brittany
Rennes
Le Mans
Orléans
Mulhouse
OCEAN
Lorient
Montbéliard
Besançon
Angers
Tours
Loire
Burgundy
Dijon
St. Nazaire
Nantes
Bourges
Loire
SWITZERLAND
Poitiers
Saône
Jura
Bay
of
Biscay
La Rochelle
Mt. Blanc
4807
Limoges
Clermont Ferrand
Lyons
Rhône
Angoulême
Auvergne
St. Étienne
Isère
Grenoble
ITALY
Valence
Massif Central
Dordogne
Cévennes
Rhône
Bordeaux
Languedoc
Orange
Garonne
Avignon
MONACO
Nice
Gascony
Nîmes
Provence
Grasse
Toulouse
Montpellier
Aix
Cannes
Bayonne
Marseilles
Toulon
Carcassonne
Gulf of Lions
Lourdes
Pyrenees
Perpignan
See page 33 for Corsica
SPAIN
ANDORRA
MEDITERRANEAN SEA

**27**

# GERMANY AND AUSTRIA

## GERMANY

**AREA** 356,910 sq km
**POPULATION** 82,000,000
**MONEY** Deutschmark

## AUSTRIA

**AREA** 83,850 sq km
**POPULATION** 8,004,000
**MONEY** Schilling

**Berlin:** *this ruined tower, next to the new tower of the Memorial Church, is left as a reminder of the destruction caused by war. It is in the city centre. Berlin is no longer divided and is once again the capital of a united Germany.*

Germany has more people than any other European country apart from Russia. Most of the 82 million Germans live in towns and cities. Several million people called 'guest workers' have come from southern Europe and Turkey to work in Germany's factories. But nowadays there is unemployment in Germany, as in other European countries, and many 'guest workers' have returned home. Among the many different goods made in Germany there are excellent cars: BMW, Ford, Mercedes, Opel, Porsche and Volkswagen.

There is also plenty of beautiful and uncrowded countryside. The north is mostly lowland. Parts of the south, such as the Black Forest, are mountainous and popular for holidays.

Germany was one country from 1870 to 1945. In 1990 it became one country again. From 1945 until 1990, it was divided into West Germany and East Germany, and there was a border fence between the two. In Berlin, the high wall that divided the city into east and west was knocked down in 1989.

**Edelweiss** *are flowers that grow high in the Alps. They can survive in thin soil on steep slopes, and do not mind being buried by snow all winter. They are a national symbol in Austria.*

**The Rhine Gorge,** *in western Germany. Castles once guarded this important river route. The River Rhine flows from Switzerland, through Germany to the Netherlands. Big barges travel between the ports and factories beside the river.*

## TRANSPORT

Germany has excellent railways. This train (above) hangs from one rail. This monorail is built over the River Wupper (near the River Ruhr) to save space.

These three stamps show a diesel engine (top left), a model of a 'hover-train' (right), and a double-decker car-transporter (left). Germany's fastest trains are labelled ICE: 'Inter-City Express'.

**AUSTRIA**: Until 1918, Austria and Hungary were linked, and together ruled a great empire which included much of Central Europe and Slovenia, Croatia and Bosnia (see page 34). But now Austria is a small, peaceful country.

In the west of Austria are the high Alps, and many tourists come to enjoy the beautiful scenery and winter sports. Busy motorways and electric railways cross the Austrian Alps to link Germany with Italy.

Most Austrians live in the lower eastern part of the country. The capital, Vienna, was once at the centre of the Austrian Empire; now it is in a corner of the country.

*Hallstatt, Austria,* is built on steep slopes which are part of the Dachstein Mountains in the eastern Alps, south-east of Salzburg. It lies beside a deep blue lake with the same name. Prehistoric remains have been found near here.

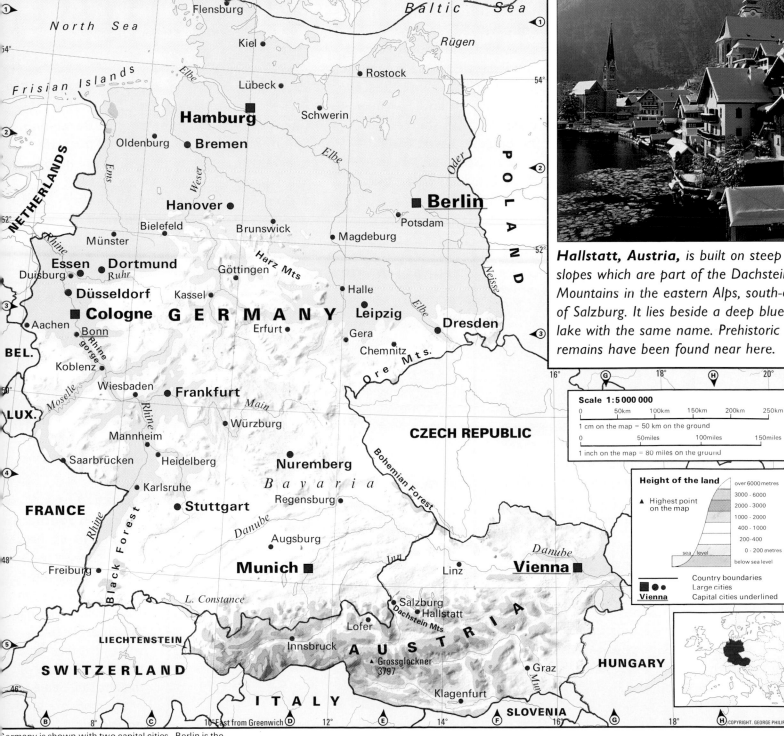

**Scale 1:5 000 000**

| 0 | 50km | 100km | 150km | 200km | 250km |

1 cm on the map = 50 km on the ground

| 0 | 50miles | 100miles | 150miles |

1 inch on the map = 80 miles on the ground

**Height of the land**

▲ Highest point on the map

- over 6000 metres
- 3000 - 6000
- 2000 - 3000
- 1000 - 2000
- 400 - 1000
- 200 - 400
- 0 - 200 metres
- below sea level

Country boundaries
■ ● ● Large cities
**Vienna** Capital cities underlined

Germany is shown with two capital cities. Berlin is the capital, but the seat of government is in Bonn.

# SPAIN AND PORTUGAL

## SPAIN

**AREA** 504,780 sq km
**POPULATION** 39,664,000
**MONEY** Peseta

## PORTUGAL

**AREA** 92,390 sq km
**POPULATION** 10,600,000
**MONEY** Escudo

Spain and Portugal are separated from the rest of Europe by the high Pyrenees Mountains. Most people travelling by land from the north reach Spain along the Atlantic or Mediterranean coasts.

The Meseta is the high plateau of central Spain. Winters are very cold, and summers are very hot. Olives and grapes are the main crops, and both Spain and Portugal export famous wines such as sherry and port. Cars are the biggest export from Spain nowadays. Both Spain and Portugal have fine cities with great churches and cathedrals, built when they were the richest countries in the world.

**Christopher Columbus' ship in Barcelona, Spain.** *Beyond the palm trees and the plaza (square) is a replica of the ship in which Columbus sailed across the Atlantic Ocean in 1492 to discover the 'New World' of the Americas. The voyage was paid for by the Queen of Spain.*

**Portuguese fishermen** *mending their nets at Tavira, on the Algarve. They continue to land sardines and other fish, but the town relies on the tourist trade for most of its income.*

## DID YOU KNOW?

*Gibraltar* is still a British colony, but it is only 6 square kilometres in area. Spain still owns two towns in Morocco: *Ceuta* and *Melilla*. Spain wants Gibraltar – and Morocco wants Ceuta and Melilla. The argument has been going on for nearly 300 years....

## THE ALHAMBRA PALACE

The Alhambra Palace, Granada. This beautiful palace was built by the Moors (Arabs from North Africa). The Moors ruled southern Spain for hundreds of years, until 1492. The Arabs brought new crops and new ideas to Europe, such as oranges, rice and sugar cane, which are still grown in Spain today.

The photo (left) of the Court of Lions shows the stone lions carved 600 years ago by Arab craftsmen.

**Village in southern Spain.** *The old houses crowd closely together, and roads are very narrow: wide enough for a donkey, but not for lorries. People whitewash their houses to reflect the rays of the hot sun. Some of the roofs are used as balconies.*

Spain is popular for holidays: the Costa Brava (Rugged Coast), Costa del Sol (Coast of the Sun) and Balearic Islands are crowded in summer. The Canary Islands belong to Spain, although they are 1150 km away, off the coast of Africa (see map page 55: square B2).

In Portugal, the Algarve coast is the most popular holiday area, along with Madeira which is far out in the Atlantic (see map page 55: B1).

Scale 1:5 000 000

1 cm on the map = 50 km on the ground

1 inch on the map = 80 miles on the ground

Height of the land

- over 6000 metres
- 3000 - 6000
- 2000 - 3000
- 1000 - 2000
- 400 - 1000
- 200 - 400
- 0 - 200 metres
- below sea level

▲ Highest point on the map

Country boundaries
Large cities
Capital cities underlined

# SWITZERLAND AND ITALY

SWITZERLAND

**AREA** 41,290 sq km
**POPULATION** 7,268,000
**MONEY** Swiss franc

***The Matterhorn** in the Swiss Alps is 4478 metres high. Glaciers helped carve its shape. Zermatt is the ski resort which gives good views of the peak.*

Italy is shaped like a boot: its toe seems to be kicking Sicily! The shape is caused by the long range of fold mountains called the Apennines. The great Roman Empire was centred on Italy, and there are many Roman ruins. Yet Italy was only united as a country less than 150 years ago. Italy has lots of big factories. The Fiat car plant in Turin is one of the largest and most modern in the world.

The south of Italy and the islands of Sicily and Sardinia have hot, dry summers. These areas are much less rich than the north. Many people have moved to the north to find work. But government projects are bringing factories and better roads.

In Switzerland, most people live in cities north of the Alps. Switzerland is one of the world's richest countries, with modern banks, offices and factories. Rivers, dams and waterfalls in the Alps are used for making hydro-electric power: trains, factories and homes in Switzerland all run on cheap electricity. Cable-cars powered by electricity take skiers and tourists high into the beautiful mountains. Switzerland holds some amazing world records (see below).

***Venice,** in north-east Italy, is a city built in the sea. Everywhere in the old town has to be reached by boat, or on foot, because the 'roads' are canals.*

## ITALIAN FOOD

**STAR Pomodori Pelati**

Large plum tomatoes are tinned (above). Many kinds of fruit are dried and used in cakes (right).

**Voiello** 145 - FUSILLI CORTI

Pasta (above) is made from Italian wheat. Spaghetti, macaroni and ravioli are pastas.

## SWISS RECORD BREAKERS!

- The longest road tunnel is the St Gotthard tunnel (16.32 km).
- The longest stairway is beside the Niesenbahn mountain railway, near Spiez. It has 11,674 steps!
- The steepest railway goes up Mount Pilatus. It has a gradient of 48%.
- Switzerland has been at peace with everyone since 1815. That's quite a record!

***Celano, in the Abruzzo region.** This is in the Apennine Mountains in central Italy. The old hill town with its castle was a safe place to live. The new town spreads over flat land which was once a lake.*

ITALY

**AREA** 301,270 sq km
**POPULATION** 58,181,000
**MONEY** Lira

**Other countries on this map:**
**VATICAN CITY** in Rome,
**SAN MARINO** within Italy,
**MALTA**, an island country south of Italy.

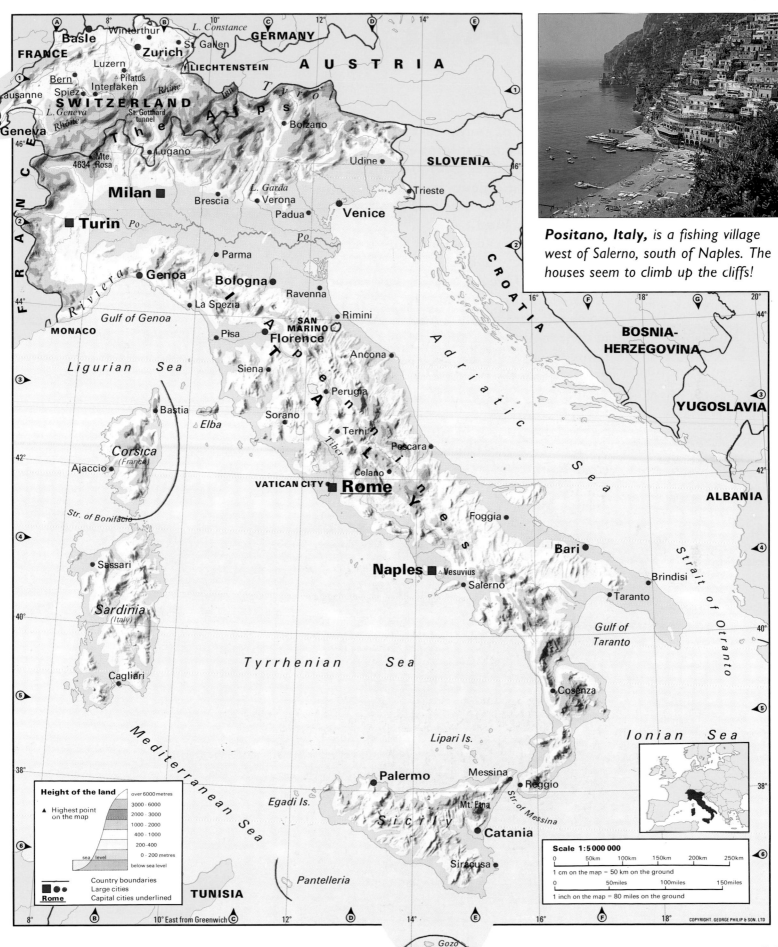

**Positano, Italy,** is a fishing village west of Salerno, south of Naples. The houses seem to climb up the cliffs!

GERMANY

AUSTRIA

LIECHTENSTEIN

Basle
Winterthur
L. Constance
St. Gallen
FRANCE
Luzern
Zurich
Bern
Pilatus
Spiez
Interlaken
Rhine
SWITZERLAND
St. Gotthard tunnel
L. Geneva
Rhone
Tyrol
The Alps
Bolzano
Geneva
Mte.
4634 Rosa
Lugano
Udine
SLOVENIA
Trieste
Milan
Brescia
L. Garda
Verona
Padua
Venice
Turin
Po
Po
Parma
Genoa
Bologna
Ravenna
Rimini
Riviera
La Spezia
SAN MARINO
CROATIA
Gulf of Genoa
Pisa
Florence
MONACO
Siena
Ancona
Ligurian Sea
Bastia
Perugia
Elba
Sorano
Adriatic Sea
BOSNIA-HERZEGOVINA
Corsica
(France)
Terni
Tiber
Ajaccio
Pescara
Celano
YUGOSLAVIA
VATICAN CITY
Rome
Appennines
Str. of Bonifacio
Foggia
ALBANIA
Sassari
Bari
Sardinia
(Italy)
Naples
Vesuvius
Brindisi
Salerno
Taranto
Cagliari
Gulf of Taranto
Strait of Otranto
Tyrrhenian Sea
Mediterranean Sea
Cosenza
Lipari Is.
Ionian Sea
Palermo
Messina
Reggio
Egadi Is.
Str. of Messina
Sicily
Mt. Etna
Catania
Pantelleria
Siracusa
TUNISIA

**Height of the land**

▲ Highest point on the map

over 6000 metres
3000 - 6000
2000 - 3000
1000 - 2000
400 - 1000
200 - 400
sea level    0 - 200 metres
below sea level

Country boundaries
Large cities
**Rome** Capital cities underlined

**Scale 1:5 000 000**

0    50km   100km   150km   200km   250km

1 cm on the map = 50 km on the ground

0         50miles      100miles     150miles

1 inch on the map = 80 miles on the ground

8°    10° East from Greenwich    12°    14°    16°    18°

COPYRIGHT. GEORGE PHILIP & SON. LTD

MALTA    Gozo
Valletta

# SOUTH-EAST EUROPE

## GREECE

**AREA** 131,990 sq km
**POPULATION** 10,510,000
**MONEY** Drachma

## BULGARIA

**AREA** 110,910 sq km
**POPULATION** 9,020,000
**MONEY** Lev

## ALBANIA

**AREA** 28,750 sq km
**POPULATION** 3,458,000
**MONEY** Lek

Most of south-east Europe is very mountainous, except near the River Danube. Farmers keep sheep and goats in the mountains and grow grain, vines and sunflowers on the lower land.

The coastlines are popular with tourists. There are many holiday resorts beside the Aegean Sea (**Greece** and **Turkey**) and the Black Sea (**Romania** and **Bulgaria**). The Romanians are building new ski villages in their mountains. All these countries are trying to develop new industries, but this is still one of the poorest parts of Europe.

**Albania** is the least-known country in all Europe: very few people visit it. No railways crossed the frontier of Albania until 1985.

**Yugoslavia** was 1 country with 2 alphabets (Latin and Cyrillic), 3 religious groups (Roman Catholic, Orthodox and Muslim), 4 languages and 6 republics. No wonder there are now problems! **Slovenia**, **Croatia**, **Macedonia** and **Bosnia-Herzegovina** are now independent countries.

**The town of Korcula, in Croatia,** is built on an island – also called Korcula – in the Adriatic Sea, north-west of Dubrovnik. In the distance are the limestone mountains of the mainland. Until 1991, Croatia was part of Yugoslavia, but after some fighting it became independent.

## THE CORINTH CANAL

A passenger liner being towed through the Corinth Canal in southern Greece. The canal was cut in 1893 and is 6.4 kilometres long. It links the Gulf of Corinth with the Aegean Sea.

**Harvest time in Romania.** The tomato harvest is being gathered by hand on a hot summer day. The horse-drawn cart will take the full boxes back to the village for distribution.

## THE DANUBE

This stamp shows a boat at the gorge on the River Danube called the Iron Gates, on the southern border of Romania. The Danube flows from Germany to a marshy delta beside the Black Sea.

| Α | Β | Γ | Δ | Ε | Ζ | Η | Θ | Ι | Κ | Λ | Μ | Ν | Ξ | Ο | Π | Ρ | Σ | Τ | Υ | Φ | Χ | Ψ | Ω |
|---|---|---|---|---|---|---|---|---|---|---|---|---|---|---|---|---|---|---|---|---|---|---|---|
| A | V/B | G | D | E | Z | E | TH | I | K | L | M | N | X | O | P | R | S | T | Y | F | CH | PS | O |

**The Greek alphabet.** *The Greeks developed their alphabet before the Romans, and they still use it. Some letters are the same as ours (A, B . . .), and some look the same but have a different sound (P, H . . .). The other letters are completely different. Some Greek letters appear in the Cyrillic alphabet, which is used in Bulgaria, Yugoslavia and Russia (see page 41). The word 'alphabet' is formed from the first two Greek letters: alpha and beta. The Greek letter for D is called 'delta'.*

**Mikonos, Greece,** *used to be a quiet village on a quiet island in the Aegean Sea. The journey from Athens was 7 hours by boat. Today, aeroplanes bring over half a million tourists to the island every year. They love the sunshine, the beaches and the boating.*

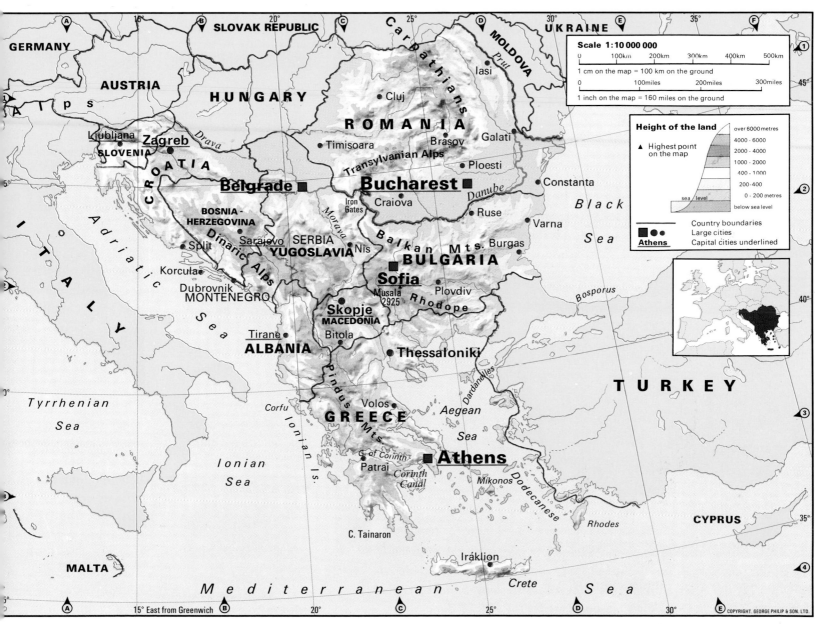

Scale 1:10 000 000

1 cm on the map = 100 km on the ground

1 inch on the map = 160 miles on the ground

Height of the land
- over 6000 metres
- 4000 - 6000
- 2000 - 4000
- 1000 - 2000
- 400 - 1000
- 200 - 400
- 0 - 200 metres
- below sea level

▲ Highest point on the map

■ Country boundaries
■ ● Large cities
Athens Capital cities underlined

**35**

# EASTERN EUROPE

## POLAND

**AREA** 312,680 sq km
**POPULATION** 38,587,000
**MONEY** Zloty

## HUNGARY

**AREA** 93,030 sq km
**POPULATION** 10,500,000
**MONEY** Forint

## UKRAINE

**AREA** 603,700 sq km
**POPULATION** 52,027,000
**MONEY** Hryvna

Poland has a coastline on the Baltic Sea. There are huge shipbuilding factories at Gdansk. There are big factories in the towns in the south, too, where there is plenty of coal. Most of the country is flat farmland, but there are magnificent mountains in the far south which are being 'rediscovered' by tourists from Western Europe.

Czechoslovakia split into two countries in 1993. The Czech Republic is west of the Slovak Republic. Both countries have beautiful hills and mountains, with fine pine trees. Skoda cars come from the Czech Republic. Further south is Hungary, which is a small, flat country. Mostly it is farmland, but Hungary also has the biggest bus factory in the world.

Polish, Czech and Slovak are all Slavic languages. Hungarian is a totally different language; it came from central Asia. Some Hungarian speakers also live in Slovakia and Romania.

***Town square in Telc, Czech Republic.*** *The historic centres of towns are carefully preserved in Eastern Europe. Some have been totally rebuilt in the old style, after wartime bombing.*

## STAMP

***Church in a lake!*** *Europe's longest river is the Volga in Russia. Dams have been built on this river, so lakes have formed behind the dams — and whole villages have vanished beneath the water. That is why there is now a church in a lake. Sadly, the dams also trap polluted water.*

***Church in Ukraine,*** *where many people are Orthodox Christians. The churches are beautiful, and the services are often very long. The Ukraine is Europe's biggest country, apart from Russia. The population is nearly as big as the UK or France.*

***Budapest, on the River Danube.*** *Buda and Pest were twin cities on either side of the River Danube. Now they have become Budapest, capital of Hungary. This picture shows old buildings on the hills of Buda.*

## BELARUS

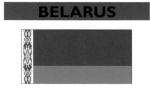

**AREA** 207,600 sq km
**POPULATION** 10,500,000
**MONEY** Rouble

Eleven countries on this map were part of the USSR until 1991. The three Baltic Republics broke away first (see box, right). Belarus (meaning 'White Russia') and little Moldova are landlocked countries. Ukraine, the largest country completely in Europe, has large areas of fertile farmland. There is plenty of coal for its steelworks. The three countries east of the Black Sea have had local wars since independence.

***Harvest-time in Poland.*** *You can still see 'horse-power' in action, though there are now far more tractors than horses. The wheat is tied into 'stooks' to dry.*

## THREE 'RE-BORN' COUNTRIES

Estonia, Latvia and Lithuania became independent countries once more in 1991. They were also independent from 1918 to 1940. They proudly show their flags on their stamps. These three countries are called 'The Baltic Republics', because they all have a coastline on the Baltic Sea. Their land is low-lying with large areas of forest. Each country is very small, and has a small population – much smaller than the population of Paris or London.

***The border of Poland (right) and the Slovak Republic (left)*** *runs along a high ridge of the Tatra Mountains. It is marked by small posts beside the footpath. The steep slopes were shaped by ice. A cable-car can take you to the border for a walk, or for skiing in winter.*

# ASIA

The world's largest continent is Asia, which stretches from the cold Arctic Ocean in the north to the warm Indian Ocean in the tropical south. Mainland Asia nearly reaches the Equator in Malaysia. Several Asian islands are on the Equator: Sumatra, Borneo and Sulawesi. In the west, Asia reaches Europe and the Mediterranean, and in the east Asia reaches the Pacific Ocean. In the centre are the high, empty plateaus of Tibet and Mongolia.

Two countries cover over half of Asia: Russia and China. India looks quite small – yet it is over ten times as big as Italy or the UK! But some of Asia's important countries are very small indeed, such as Lebanon and Israel in south-west Asia (Middle East); Singapore and Brunei in south-east Asia (Far East).

Over half the world's population lives in Asia. The coastal areas of south and east Asia are the most crowded parts. Seven of the 'top ten' most populated countries in the world are in Asia: China, India, Indonesia, Russia, Japan, Bangladesh and Pakistan (see page 9).

**This Buddhist shrine** is like many found in Nepal. It has been decorated with prayer flags and painted eyes.

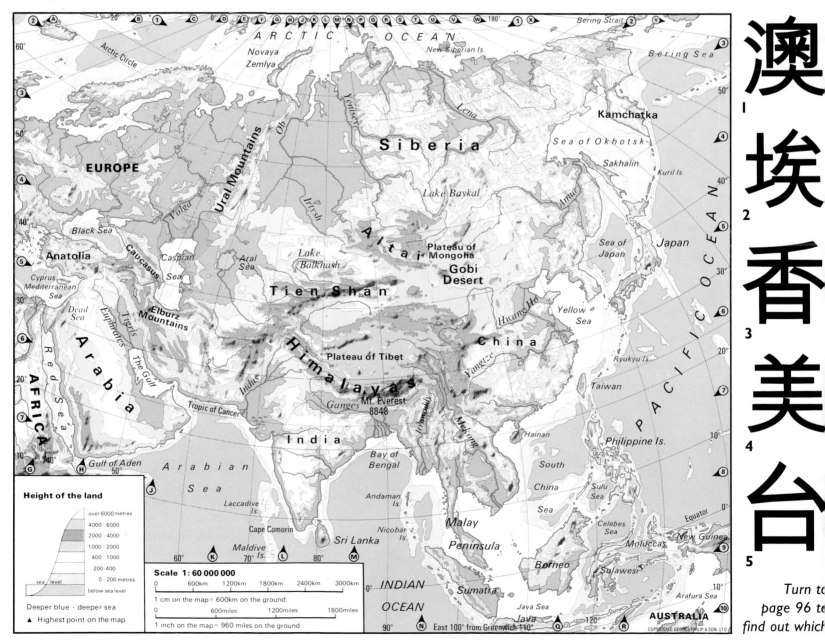

**Height of the land**

- over 6000 metres
- 4000 - 6000
- 2000 - 4000
- 1000 - 2000
- 400 - 1000
- 200 - 400
- 0 - 200 metres
- sea level
- below sea level

Deeper blue - deeper sea

▲ Highest point on the map

**Scale 1 : 60 000 000**

| 0 | 600km | 1200km | 1800km | 2400km | 3000km |

1 cm on the map = 600km on the ground

| 0 | 600miles | 1200miles | 1800miles |

1 inch on the map = 960 miles on the ground

澳埃香美台

Turn to page 96 to find out which

## ASIA FACTS

**AREA** 44,387,000 sq km (including Asiatic Russia)

**HIGHEST POINT** Mount Everest (Nepal/China), 8848 metres (A *world record* as well as an Asian record.)

**LOWEST POINT** Shores of Dead Sea (Israel/Jordan), 400 metres below sea level
(A *world record* as well as an Asian record.)

**LONGEST RIVERS** Yangtze (China), 6380 km; Yenisey (Russia), 5540 km

**BIGGEST COUNTRY** Russia, 17,075,000 sq km
(A *world record* as well as an Asian record.)

**SMALLEST COUNTRY** The Maldives, 298 sq km

**LARGEST LAKE** Caspian Sea 360,700 sq km
(A *world record* as well as an Asian record.)
The Caspian Sea is shared by five countries – which are they? (Answers on page 96.)

**Himalayan Mountains, Nepal.** *The photograph shows the peaks of the Annapurnas rising above the cloud. Annapurna I is 8091 metres high and was first climbed in 1950. The other four peaks in the group are over 7500 metres high. The Himalayas are the world's highest mountain range, with all the world's 'top ten' highest peaks, including Mount Everest.*

洲及港國灣

*...untries are ...Chinese ...cript here.*

# RUSSIA AND NEIGHBOURS

## RUSSIA

**AREA** 17,075,000 sq km
**POPULATION** 148,385,000
**MONEY** Rouble

## UZBEKISTAN

**AREA** 447,400 sq km
**POPULATION** 22,833,000
**MONEY** Som

## TURKMENISTAN

**AREA** 488,100 sq km
**POPULATION** 4,100,000
**MONEY** Manat

**R**ussia stretches across two continents, Europe and Asia. Most of the people live in the European part, west of the Ural Mountains. Some people have moved east to new towns in Siberia.

Because Russia is so huge, there are many different climates and almost all crops can be grown. The far north is snow-covered for most of the year (see page 88). Further south is the largest forest in the world – a vast area of coniferous trees stretching from the Baltic Sea to the Sea of Okhotsk in the far east. Grassy plains, called the steppes, are found south of the forest. In some parts, grain is grown on huge farms. Russia also has huge deposits of many different minerals and can supply most of the needs of its many different factories.

The republics of central Asia are mostly in a desert area – hot in summer but bitterly cold in winter. With irrigation, crops such as sugar-cane and cotton grow well.

***St Basil's cathedral, Moscow,*** *is at one end of Red Square. It is famous for its brightly coloured domes: each one is different. In the background are the domes and towers of buildings inside the Kremlin walls. 'Kremlin' means 'fortress'. The Moscow Kremlin has a cathedral and offices of the government of Russia.*

***In Uzbekistan,*** *people still use traditional looms like this one, for weaving silk, cotton and wool – but there is modern industry as well. Uzbekistan is one of the 15 'new' countries created when the USSR broke up in 1991. Can you name them? (Page 37 will help; answers on page 96.)*

## THE ARAL SEA . . .

*. . . is getting smaller.* These ships were once in the Aral Sea, but are now on dry land. This salty lake is drying up because rivers do not refill it with enough water. The water is used to irrigate fields instead.

***Siberia*** *has the world's largest forest. It stretches from the Ural Mountains to the far east of Russia. Most of the trees are conifers. They can survive the Siberian winters, which are long and extremely cold.*

# А Б В Г Д Е Ё Ж З И Й К Л М Н О П Р С Т У Ф Х Ц Ч Ш Щ Ю Я

A B V G D E YO ZH Z I Y K L M N O P R S T U F KH TS CH SH SHCH YU YA

*The Cyrillic alphabet.* Russian is written in the Cyrillic alphabet. This is partly based on Latin letters (the same as English letters) and partly on Greek letters (see page 35).

The alphabet was invented centuries ago by St Cyril, so that the Russian church could show it was separate from both the Roman and the Greek churches. In Cyrillic, R is written P, and S is written C. So the Metro is written МЕТРО.

Can you understand this message? Use the key above: **ХАБАРОВСК** (square S4) is on the River **АМУР** (see square R3 on the map).

Now can you write Volga (the river) in Russian? Check your answer with the postage stamp on page 36. Now work out what the sign on the railway carriage (right) says. It's not as hard as it looks!

## TRANS-SIBERIAN RAILWAY

It takes a week to cross Russia by train, and you must change your watch seven times. Here is the distance chart and timetable (only the main stops are shown).

**МОСКВА-ВЛАДИВОСТОК**

This is the plate on the side of the train. The translation is on page 96. This is one of the world's most exciting train journeys.

| DISTANCE (IN KM) | TOWN | TIME (IN MOSCOW) | DAY |
|---|---|---|---|
| 0 | Moscow | 15:05 | 1 |
| 957 | Kirov | 04:00 | 2 |
| 1818 | Yekaterinburg | 16:25 | 2 |
| 2716 | Omsk | 03:13 | 3 |
| 3343 | Novosibirsk | 10:44 | 3 |
| 4104 | Krasnoyarsk | 22:31 | 3 |
| 5184 | Irkutsk | 16:23 | 4 |
| 5647 | Ulan Ude | 00:02 | 5 |
| 6204 | Chita | 09:23 | 5 |
| 7313 | Skovorodino | 05:20 | 6 |
| 8531 | Khabarovsk | 01:10 | 7 |
| 9297 | Vladivostok | 13:30* | 7 |

\* This is 20:30 local time in Vladivostok.

At these stations, there is time for a quick walk – and some bartering. But don't forget to allow another week to come back!

Scale 1: 45 000 000

1 cm on the map = 450 km on the ground

1 inch on the map = 720 miles on the ground

**Height of the land**

| | |
|---|---|
| ▲ Highest point on the map | over 6000 metres |
| | 4000 - 6000 |
| | 2000 - 4000 |
| | 1000 - 2000 |
| | 400 - 1000 |
| | 200 - 400 |
| | 0 - 200 metres |
| | below sea level |

Country boundaries
Large cities
**Moscow** Capital city underlined

More details of European Russia are shown on page 37

**41**

# MIDDLE EAST

**AREA** 2,149,690 sq km
**POPULATION** 18,395,000
**MONEY** Saudi riyal

## JORDAN

**AREA** 89,210 sq km
**POPULATION** 5,547,000
**MONEY** Jordan dinar

## IRAN

**AREA** 1,648,000 sq km
**POPULATION** 68,885,000
**MONEY** Rial

The 'Middle East' is another name for 'south-west Asia'. It is the part of Asia which is closest to Europe and Africa. In fact, it is the only place where three continents meet. Turkey is partly in Europe and mostly in Asia. Of all the countries on this map, Turkey and Iran have the most people.

Most of the Middle East is semi-desert or desert. Yet many great civilizations have existed here, such as the Assyrian, the Babylonian and the Persian. Their monuments are found in the fertile valleys of the largest rivers, the Tigris and the Euphrates.

Scarce water is used to irrigate crops in some places. In others, herds of sheep and goats are kept. Dates from Iraq come from desert oases; oranges come from irrigated land in Israel. So much water is being taken from the River Jordan that the Dead Sea is getting smaller. Some countries make fresh water from salt water, but it is expensive.

***Craft stall in Istanbul.*** *Craft industries still thrive in Turkey, and throughout the Middle East. The metal plates and pots were hammered out and decorated by hand. Europe and Asia meet at Istanbul, which used to be called Constantinople.*

## IRAQ

**AREA** 438,320 sq km
**POPULATION** 20,184,000
**MONEY** Iraqi dinar

## STAMPS

***Progress in Qatar*** *is shown by the highways and high-rise office blocks being built with money from oil.*

***Yemen:*** *an Arab scribe makes beautiful writing into an art form on this stamp.*

## HOLY CITIES OF THE MIDDLE EAST

**Jerusalem:** a Jewish boy's Bar Mitzvah ceremony at the West Wall ('Wailing Wall'). The huge stones (in the background, on the right) are all that remains of the Jewish temple. Jerusalem is a holy city for Jews, Christians and Muslims. People of all three religions live here and many pilgrims and tourists visit the city.

**Mecca:** crowds of pilgrims surround the Kaaba (the huge black stone, right) inside the Great Mosque. Mecca is the holiest city of Islam as it is where the prophet Mohammed was born. Muslims try to come to worship here at least once in their lifetime. But wherever they are, they face towards Mecca when they pray.

The Middle East has changed dramatically in the last 50 years. Oil was found beneath the Arabian desert and around The Gulf. At the same time, oil was in great demand in Europe and all over the world. The sale of oil has made some countries very rich, especially Saudi Arabia, Kuwait and Qatar. Often the rulers have benefited most, but they have also used the money to build schools, hospitals, fine roads and office blocks (see Qatar stamp). The 'oil boom' has meant that many foreign workers have come to these countries.

**Muscat** is the capital city and chief port of Oman. The city is surrounded by rock desert and dry mountains. The Sultan has his palace here.

**Camels in the desert** of the United Arab Emirates – a view that has not changed for centuries. Only camels can be kept in such dry conditions.

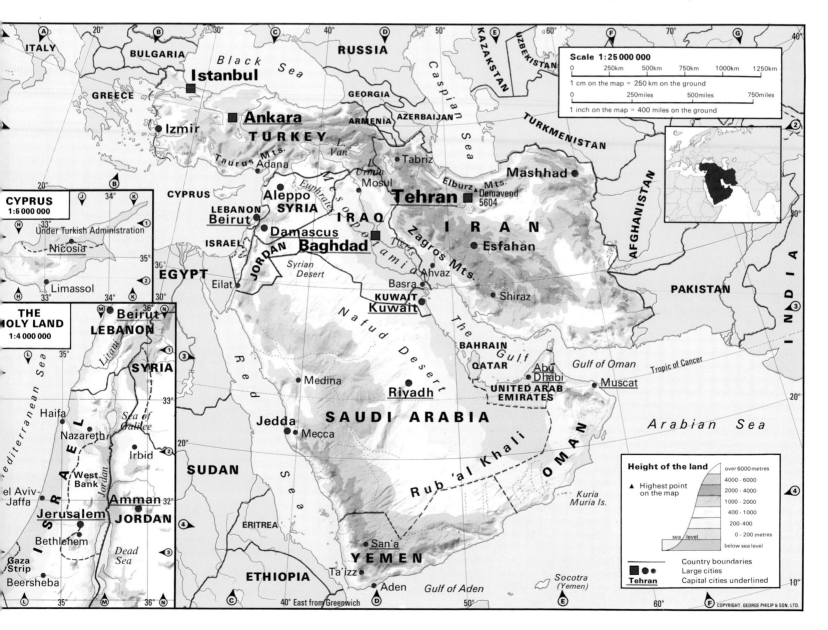

# SOUTH ASIA

### INDIA

**AREA** 3,287,590 sq km
**POPULATION** 942,989,000
**MONEY** Indian rupee
**CAPITAL** New Delhi

### PAKISTAN

**AREA** 796,100 sq km
**POPULATION** 143,595,000
**MONEY** Pakistan rupee
**CAPITAL** Islamabad

### SRI LANKA

**AREA** 65,610 sq km
**POPULATION** 18,359,000
**MONEY** Sri Lankan rupee

The world's highest mountains appear on this map, including Mount Everest. The Himalayas form a great mountain chain which joins on to other high mountain areas, such as the Hindu Kush.

More than 1200 million people live in south Asia. The deserts and mountains do not have many people, but the river valleys, plains and plateaus are crowded.

**Afghanistan**, **Bhutan** and **Nepal** are rugged, mountainous countries.

**Bangladesh** is very different: it is mostly flat, low-lying land where the great rivers Ganges and Brahmaputra reach the sea.

**Pakistan** is a desert country, but the River Indus is used to irrigate crops.

**India** is the largest country. It stretches 3300 kilometres from the Himalayas to Cape Comorin. Until 1947, Pakistan and Bangladesh were part of the Indian Empire, ruled by Britain.

**Sri Lanka** (formerly called Ceylon) is a mountainous island off the coast of India.

**The Maldives** are a chain of low, flat, coral islands in the Indian Ocean.

***Wool for carpets.*** *This lady in northern India is winding wool which will be used to make carpets. She sits in the courtyard of her house, where the ploughs and pots and pans are also kept.*

### TEA

**Tea** is an important crop in the hills of Sri Lanka where nights are cool, and there is plenty of rain. Women pick the new young leaves from the bushes (as shown on the stamp). The leaves are then dried

and crushed, and packed into large tea-chests for storage. 'Ceylon Tea' is one of Sri Lanka's most important exports. Where does the tea you drink come from?

**INDIAN FOOD**
Most Indians are vegetarians. They like hot and spicy food. How many ingredients in this picture can you name?
(Answers on page 96.)

### AFGHANISTAN

**AREA** 652,090 sq km
**POPULATION** 19,509,000
**MONEY** Afghani

### NEPAL

**AREA** 140,800 sq km
**POPULATION** 21,953,000
**MONEY** Nepalese rupee

RELIGION is very important in the lives of people in south Asia.

**Hinduism** is the oldest religion, and most people in India and Nepal are Hindus.

**Buddhism** began in India, but only Sri Lanka and Bhutan are mainly Buddhist today.

**Islam** is the religion of the majority of people in Afghanistan, Pakistan and Bangladesh.

Many **Sikhs** live in northern India; there are also **Christian** groups in all these countries.

**Rice** is an important food crop in south Asia. It grows best where the land is flat, and where the weather is hot and wet. In a good year, rice grows in the wet fields and is ready for harvesting after four or five months. If the monsoon fails and there is a drought, the seedlings will shrivel up. If the rice crop fails, many people go hungry. Where irrigation is available, the farmer can control the water supply and may be able to grow two rice crops a year.

*Planting rice, Kashmir, India.* These men are planting out rice seedlings in the wet soil.

## MOUNT EVEREST

**Mount Everest** is the world's highest mountain – 8848 metres above sea level. It was not climbed until 1953.

Everest is on the border of Nepal and Tibet (now part of China) – find it on the map in square D2. It is called 'Sagarmatha' in Nepalese, and in Chinese it is 'Qomolangma' (Queen of Mountains).

The photograph shows a glacier below the icy summit, and the bare rock that climbers have to cross. At this height, the air has little oxygen, so climbing is very hard.

# SOUTH-EAST ASIA

### PHILIPPINES

**AREA** 300,000 sq km
**POPULATION** 67,167,000
**MONEY** Peso

### THAILAND

**AREA** 513,120 sq km
**POPULATION** 58,432,000
**MONEY** Baht

### SINGAPORE

**AREA** 618 sq km
**POPULATION** 2,990,000
**MONEY** Singapore dollar

*Singapore is the world's most crowded country. Old houses (in the foreground) are being pulled down and new skyscrapers are replacing them.*

The Equator crosses South-east Asia, so it is always hot. Heavy tropical rainstorms are common. The mainland and most of the islands are very mountainous.

**Indonesia** is the biggest country. It used to be called the Dutch East Indies.

**The Philippines** is another large group of islands, south of China. They were Spanish until 1898.

**Malaysia** includes part of the mainland and most of northern Borneo.

**Brunei** is a very small but a very rich country on the island of Borneo.

**Burma (Myanmar)** was part of the Indian Empire. It became independent in 1948.

**Vietnam, Laos** and **Cambodia** were once called French Indo-China.

**Thailand** has always been independent, and has a king.

***Rice terraces, Bali.*** *Rice grows on terraces cut into the mountainside in Bali. Each terrace is sown and harvested by hand. Bali is a small island east of Java. Some people claim that it is the most beautiful island of Indonesia, and in all the world!*

## GROWING RICE

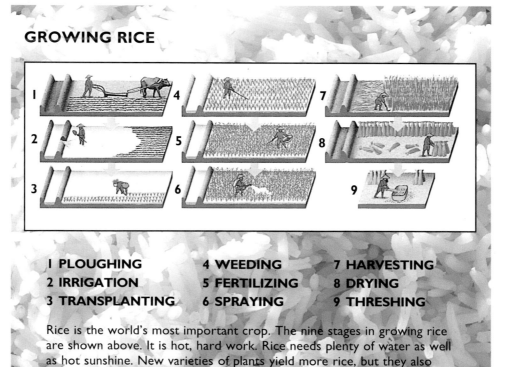

| | | |
|---|---|---|
| 1 PLOUGHING | 4 WEEDING | 7 HARVESTING |
| 2 IRRIGATION | 5 FERTILIZING | 8 DRYING |
| 3 TRANSPLANTING | 6 SPRAYING | 9 THRESHING |

Rice is the world's most important crop. The nine stages in growing rice are shown above. It is hot, hard work. Rice needs plenty of water as well as hot sunshine. New varieties of plants yield more rice, but they also need more fertilizer, more water and more care.

***Floating market in Thailand.*** *Farmers bring their fruit and vegetables by boat to a market at Damnoen Saduak, to the west of Bangkok. Fish are cooked on some of the boats and sold for lunch.*

The mountains of South-east Asia are covered with thick tropical forest (look at the stamp of Laos). These areas are very difficult to reach and have few people. The large rivers are important routes inland. Their valleys and deltas are very crowded indeed.

Java, Bali and Singapore are among the most crowded islands in the world – yet several bigger islands, such as Sulawesi and Borneo, have very small populations.

**Laos.** Elephants carry huge logs from the jungle. Laos was called Lanxang – 'land of a million elephants'.

**Vietnam.** These young children are learning to draw a map of their country.

**Malaysia** has a hot, wet climate. Pineapples grow well here. Some are tinned and exported.

**Indonesia** is mainly an Islamic country. The moon and star (seen here above a mosque) are traditional symbols of Islam.

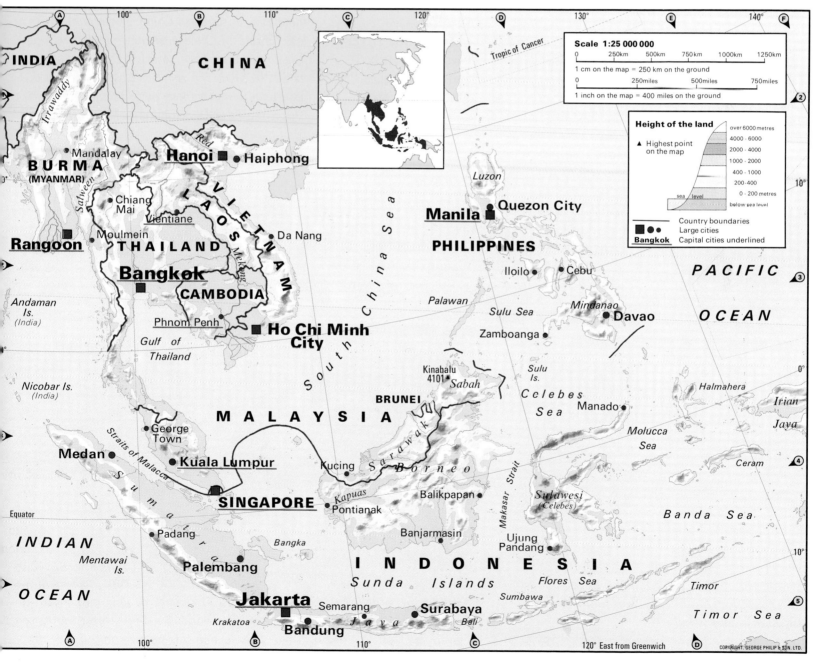

# CHINA AND NEIGHBOURS

## CHINA

**AREA** 9,596,960 sq km
**POPULATION** 1,226,944,000
**MONEY** Yuan

## MONGOLIA

**AREA** 1,566,500 sq km
**POPULATION** 2,408,000
**MONEY** Tugrik

**Building a reservoir.**
*Everybody, male and female, pulls a heavy cart of rocks to make a new dam across a river. The dam will provide water for power and for irrigation – and it will control flooding too.*

**C**hina has over a billion people (1,226,944,000) – more than any other country in the world. The map shows that there are many high mountains in China, such as the huge plateau of Tibet and the rugged mountains of the south-west where the Giant Pandas live. Not many people live in these mountains, nor in the deserts of the north, near Mongolia.

So the lower land of eastern China is very crowded indeed. Rice grows well south of the River Yangtze. North of the Yangtze, where the winters are colder, wheat and maize are important food crops, but it is hard to grow enough.

**North Korea** is a Communist country. It separated from South Korea in the Korean War in 1953.

**South Korea** has over 44 million people – more than Canada and Australia put together!

**Taiwan** is an island country which used to be called Formosa, or Nationalist China. It is not Communist and is not part of China.

## STAMP

**Mongolia** *has its own language and script. It is a huge country with many deserts.*

**China's amazing mountains.** *The photograph shows the amazing shapes of the limestone mountains in southern China. The mountains that look 'unreal' in Chinese paintings really are real! It is almost impossible to travel through this area except by boat. The rain has slowly dissolved the limestone to make these picturesque mountains. This is the River Li, a tributary of the Yangtze.*

## NORTH KOREA

**AREA** 120,540 sq km
**POPULATION** 23,931,000
**MONEY** N. Korean won

## SOUTH KOREA

**AREA** 99,020 sq km
**POPULATION** 45,088,000
**MONEY** S. Korean won

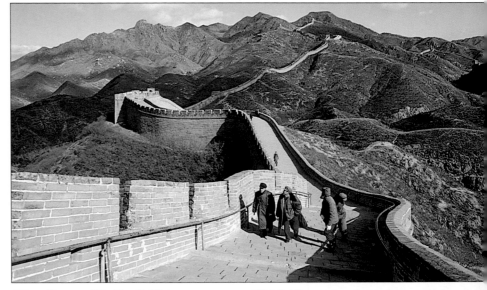

**The Great Wall of China** *was over 5000 kilometres long (see map) – by far the longest man-made structure in the world. Building started 2000 years ago to keep China's enemies out. This section has been repaired recently.*

## HONG KONG

Most of Hong Kong was part of China until 1898 and is Chinese again from 1997 onwards. For 99 years the British ruled Hong Kong. These photographs show tall skyscrapers, which stand on hillsides. Nearly 6 million people live in this small, crowded territory. Travel is a problem. Double-deck trams and buses can carry lots of people.

# FACT BOX

- One out of every five people in the world is Chinese.
- The Chinese invented the compass, paper and printing.
- The Chinese have been eating with chopsticks for 3000 years!
- The place furthest from the open sea is in China: the Dzungarian Desert, which is 2400 km from the sea.
- Tibet is the highest plateau in the world. Its average height is nearly 5000 metres above sea level.

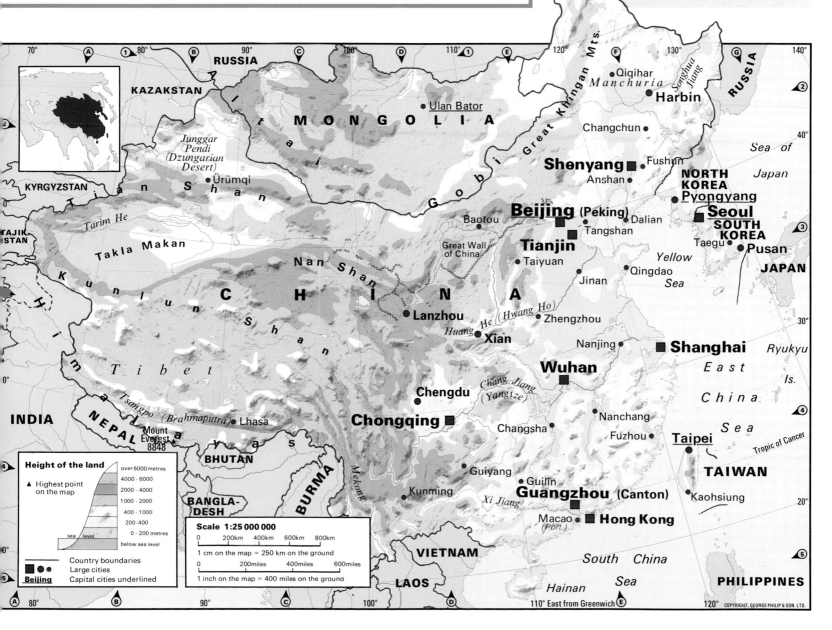

**Height of the land**

| | |
|---|---|
| over 6000 metres | |
| 4000 - 6000 | |
| 2000 - 4000 | |
| 1000 - 2000 | |
| 400 - 1000 | |
| 200 - 400 | |
| 0 - 200 metres | |
| below sea level | |

▲ Highest point on the map

Country boundaries
■ ● ● Large cities
**Beijing** Capital cities underlined

**Scale 1:25 000 000**

0   200km   400km   600km   800km
1 cm on the map = 250 km on the ground

0   200miles   400miles   600miles
1 inch on the map = 400 miles on the ground

COPYRIGHT: GEORGE PHILIP & SON. LTD.

# JAPAN

## KANSAI AIRPORT

*This new airport serves Osaka and Kobe. The runway and terminal are on land reclaimed from the sea, as flat land is scarce in Japan.*

*Osaka's old airport was in the city. The new airport is 1 km offshore. Expressways link it to the city. Can you match the photo and the map on the stamp? (HINT: look at one upside down!)*

**J**apan is quite a small country: it is smaller than France or Spain. Canada is 27 times as big as Japan! But Japan has a big population – about 125,000,000. This is over twice as many people as France, and five times as many as Canada.

People talk of the 'Japanese miracle'. This small country is mostly mountains, has very few mines and hardly any oil, yet it has become the world's biggest producer of televisions, radios, stereo hi-fis, cameras, trucks, ships and many other things. Japanese cars and computers are admired throughout the world.

There are booming cities in the south of Japan, with highly skilled, hard-working people. Many of them live in the city suburbs and travel to work in overcrowded trains. Most Japanese families have small, space-saving homes. The main room is usually a living room by day, then the beds are unrolled for the night and packed away next morning. But away from the cities, most of Japan is still beautiful and peaceful.

**Mount Fuji, with tea fields in the foreground.** *Mount Fuji (Fuji-san) is Japan's most famous mountain. It is an old volcano, 3776 metres high. In winter, the upper slopes are covered with snow. Tea is important in Japan. It is usually drunk as 'green tea' and often with great ceremony.*

## JAPAN

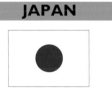

**AREA** 377,800 sq km
**POPULATION** 125,156,000
**MONEY** Yen
**CAPITAL** Tokyo
**MAIN ISLAND** Honshu

**Cherry blossom time at a garden in Nagano,** *in the centre of Honshu Island. Japan has many gardens which are especially beautiful in spring.*

## STAMP

**Horyu Temple, at Nara.** *The beautiful temple on the right is called a pagoda. Japanese pagodas are carefully preserved. Their unusual shape originally came partly from Indian and partly from Chinese temples.*

**Bullet train.** *Japan's 'bullet trains' go like a bullet from a gun! The trains run on new tracks with no sharp curves to slow them down. They provide a superb service except when there is an earthquake warning. When that happens, the trains have to go more slowly, to be safe.*

Most Japanese live on Honshu, the largest island. Hokkaido, the northernmost island, is much less crowded. Winters are very cold and even the summers are too cold for growing rice. But in the south of Japan, rice is the main food crop. Some of the hillsides look like giant steps, because they are terraced to make flat fields. Many mountains in Japan are volcanoes: 54 are active and there are over 100 others.

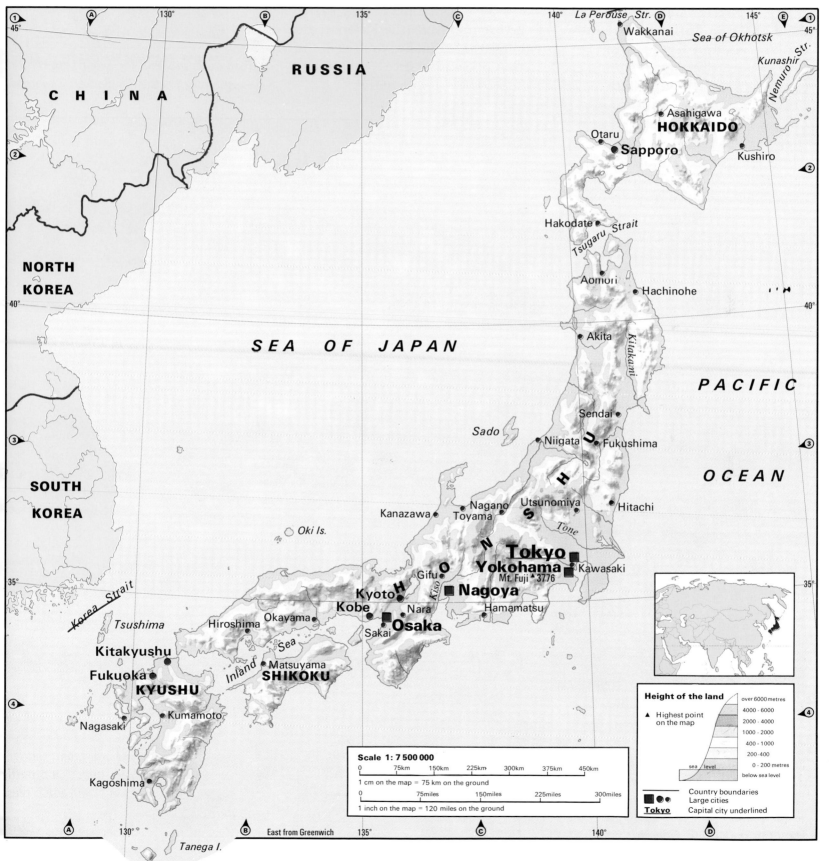

# AFRICA

**M**ost of the countries of Africa have quite small populations – except for Nigeria and Egypt. But everywhere the population is growing fast. It is difficult to provide enough schools and clinics for all the children and there are not enough good jobs.

Imagine travelling southwards across Africa, along the 20°E line of longitude. You start in Libya. Your first 1000 kilometres will be across the great Sahara Desert (where you must travel in winter) – sand, rock and the high rugged Tibesti Mountains. Then you reach thorn bushes, in the semi-desert Sahel area of Chad.

By 15°N you are into savanna – very long grass and scattered trees. You cross the country known as CAR for short. The land becomes greener and at about 5°N you reach the equatorial rainforest . . . a real jungle! You are now in Zaïre.

Then the same story happens in reverse – savanna in Angola; then semi-desert (the Kalahari and the Karoo). Finally, you reach the coast of South Africa – a journey of nearly 8000 kilometres.

*Railways* are vital for exports from Africa – especially for the 'landlocked' countries.

***Children in Ghana.*** *Everywhere in Africa, there are lots of children. The fathers of these children are fishermen: in the background you can see nets drying and big dug-out canoes. The canoes are made from the huge trees of the rainforest, and can cope with big waves in the Gulf of Guinea.*

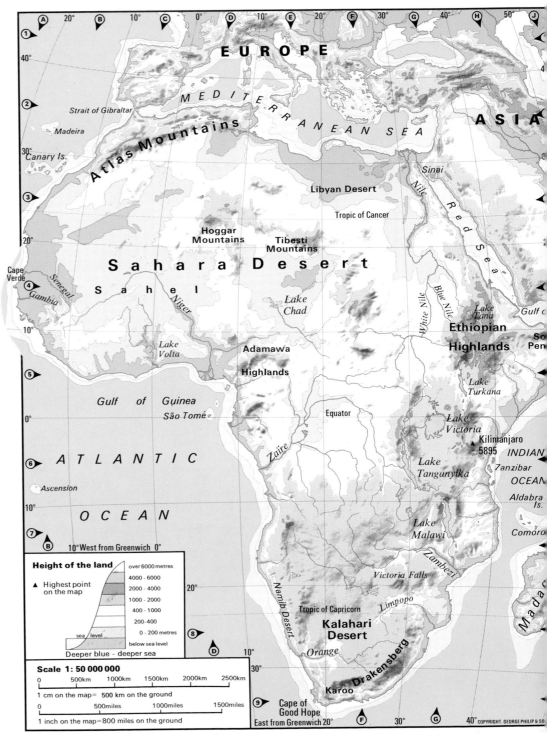

Height of the land

over 6000 metres
4000 - 6000
2000 - 4000
1000 - 2000
400 - 1000
200 - 400
0 - 200 metres
below sea level
Deeper blue - deeper sea

▲ Highest point on the map

sea level

Scale 1: 50 000 000

0   500km   1000km   1500km   2000km   2500km

1 cm on the map = 500 km on the ground

0   500miles   1000miles   1500miles

1 inch on the map = 800 miles on the ground

## ORIGIN OF COUNTRY NAMES

**CHAD** Named from Lake Chad
**GAMBIA, NIGER, NIGERIA** From big rivers
**GHANA, BENIN, MALI** Names of great
empires in West Africa a long time ago
**IVORY COAST** Ivory, from the tusks of
elephants, was traded along this coast
**NAMIBIA** From the Namib Desert
**SIERRA LEONE** 'Lion Mountain' (Portuguese)
**TANZANIA** From *Tanganyika* (the
mainland) and the island of *Zanzibar*

*The pyramids of Egypt are tombs built by slaves over 4000 years ago. The picture shows the largest, which are at Giza, near Cairo. They are still the largest buildings in the whole of Africa. They are near the River Nile, in the Sahara Desert.*

## COINS OF AFRICA

All the 55 countries of Africa have their own banknotes and stamps. Most countries have coins as well. Pictures on the coins usually show something about the country. The 5 Bututs coin from The Gambia (above) shows a fine sailing ship. There is Arabic writing because many people are Muslims. The 10 Kobo coin from Nigeria shows palm trees.

## AFRICAN FACTS

**AREA** 30,319,000 sq km
**HIGHEST POINT** Mount Kilimanjaro
(Tanzania), 5895 metres
**LOWEST POINT** Shores of Lake Assal
(Djibouti), 155 metres below sea level
**LONGEST RIVER** Nile, 6670 km
(also a world record)
**LARGEST LAKE** Lake Victoria
(East Africa), 69,484 sq km
**BIGGEST COUNTRY** Sudan, 2,505,810 sq km
**SMALLEST COUNTRIES**
Mainland: Gambia, 11,300 sq km;
Islands: Seychelles, 455 sq km (see page 9)

At the time of going to press, the government of Zaïre had been overthrown by rebels who planned to rename the country 'The Democratic Republic of the Congo'.

# NORTH AFRICA

### EGYPT

**AREA** 1,001,450 sq km
**POPULATION** 64,100,000
**MONEY** Egyptian pound

### MOROCCO

**AREA** 446,550 sq km
**POPULATION** 26,857,000
**MONEY** Moroccan dirham

### MALI

**AREA** 1,240,190 sq km
**POPULATION** 10,700,000
**MONEY** CFA franc

**M**ost of North Africa is desert – but not all. The coastlines and mountains of north-west Africa get winter rain: good crops are grown and the coasts of Tunisia and Morocco are popular with tourists.

All these countries are Islamic. Morocco has the oldest university in the world: the Islamic University in Fez. The largest country in Africa is the Sudan. A civil war has continued for years because the people of the far south do not want to be ruled by the Islamic north.

People can live in the desert if there is water. Some modern settlements have been built deep in the desert where there are valuable minerals, and water is pumped from underground. These minerals are the main reason why some countries are richer than others. Algeria and Libya have plenty of oil beneath the desert. But the countries in the southern part of the Sahara are among the poorest in the world. They had severe famines in the 1970s and 1980s.

*A market near Timbuktu, in Mali,* is a place to meet as well as to trade. People bring the goods they hope to sell in locally made baskets or in re-used cartons which they balance on their heads.

### SUDAN

**AREA** 2,505,810 sq km
**POPULATION** 29,980,000
**MONEY** Sudanese dinar

## SUEZ CANAL

This old print shows the procession of ships through the Suez Canal at its opening in December 1869. The canal links the Mediterranean with the Red Sea (see map: G1). It was dug in 1859–69 by Arabs, organized by a Frenchman, Ferdinand de Lesseps. Before the canal opened, the route by sea from Europe to India and the Far East was around the whole of Africa.

*Oasis near Lake Djerid, Tunisia. Water is just below the ground, so date palms can grow well. But in the background, great sand dunes loom on the skyline. If they advance, they may cover the oasis.*

*A tall story!* Trees can be very useful in so many ways – this man is looking for the only giraffes in North and West Africa. They were brought to Niger by a German who thought the local people could look after the giraffes and make money from tourists!

**Egypt** has the biggest population of any North African country. Its capital, Cairo, is one of the biggest cities in the world. The River Nile brings water to the valley and delta. The land is carefully farmed (with irrigation) and crowded with people; the rest of Egypt is almost empty. The world population map on page 10 makes the contrast very clear. The map below shows that part of the desert is below sea level.

The lack of rain has helped to preserve many of the marvellous monuments, palaces and tombs built by the ancient Egyptians. The pyramids at Giza, near Cairo, are 4500 years old (see page 53). They are the only one of the Seven Wonders of the ancient world still surviving.

## THE SAHARA DESERT

The Sahara is the biggest desert in the world. It is over 8 million sq km in size. From west to east it is over 5000 km; from north to south it extends about 2000 km and it is still growing.

**THE HOTTEST SHADE TEMPERATURE** ever recorded, 58°C, was in Al Aziziyah, Libya, in 1922.

**THE SUNNIEST PLACE** in the world, over 4300 hours of sunshine per year, is in the eastern Sahara.

**THE HIGHEST SAND DUNES** in the world, 430 metres high, are in central Algeria (see below).

**THE LONGEST RIVER** in the world is the River Nile, 6670 km long.

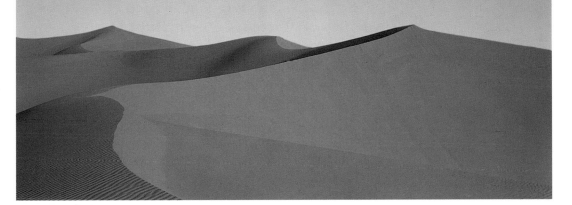

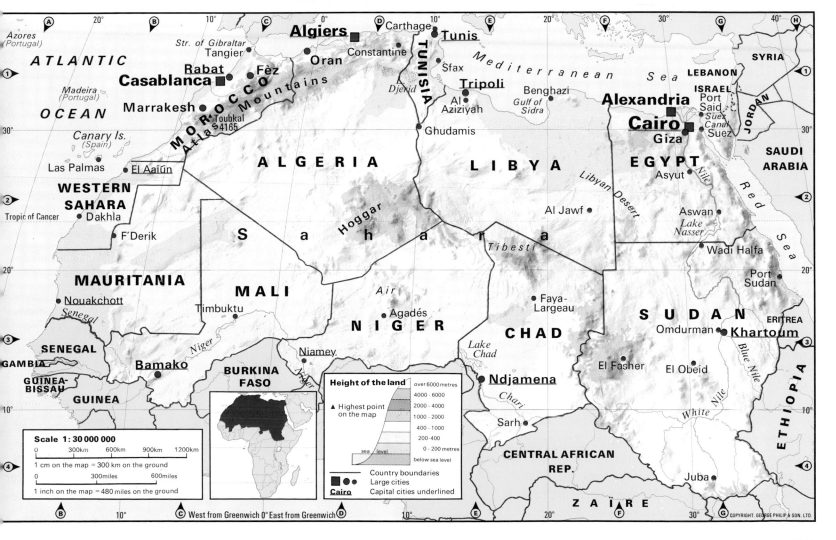

Height of the land

over 6000 metres
4000 - 6000
2000 - 4000
1000 - 2000
400 - 1000
200 - 400
0 - 200 metres
below sea level

▲ Highest point on the map

Scale 1: 30 000 000

0   300km  600km  900km  1200km
1 cm on the map = 300 km on the ground

0        300miles      600miles
1 inch on the map = 480 miles on the ground

■●● Country boundaries
● Large cities
**Cairo** Capital cities underlined

West from Greenwich 0° East from Greenwich

COPYRIGHT. GEORGE PHILIP & SON. LTD.

**55**

# WEST AFRICA

## NIGERIA

**AREA** 923,770 sq km
**POPULATION** 88,515,000
**MONEY** Naira

## THE GAMBIA

**AREA** 11,300 sq km
**POPULATION** 1,144,000
**MONEY** Dalasi

## IVORY COAST

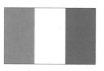

**AREA** 322,460 sq km
**POPULATION** 14,271,000
**MONEY** CFA franc

There are lots of countries in West Africa. In the last 300 years, European countries grabbed parts of the coastline and later they took over the inland areas as well. Now, all the countries are independent, but still use the language of those who once ruled them. English, French, Spanish or Portuguese is spoken. Many Africans speak a European language as well as one or more African languages.

Nigeria is the largest and most important country in West Africa. It has over 88 million people – more than any other African country. Although English is the official language, there are about 240 others in Nigeria!

In many parts of West Africa, there is rapid progress. Most children now go to primary school, and the main cities have television and airports. But many people are still very poor. Civil war has made poverty much worse in some countries – for example, in Sierra Leone and Liberia.

**Village in Cameroon:** building houses with mud for the walls and tall grass for thatch. These materials are free and the homes are less hot than those with imported corrugated iron roofs.

## SIERRA LEONE

**AREA** 71,740 sq km
**POPULATION** 4,467,000
**MONEY** Leone

**Market day, Nigeria.** Red peppers for sale in Benin City, in southern Nigeria. Red peppers are very popular in West Africa – they give a strong flavour in cooking. Markets are important in both towns and villages throughout Africa.

### BIRDS

West Africa has many brightly coloured birds which live in the forest and savanna. These stamps show a Grey Headed Bush-Shrike (left) and a Variable Sunbird (below).

West Africa is also home for part of the year to many birds that are familiar in Europe. Swallows, warblers, swifts and many others migrate to Africa during the European winter.

**Women pounding yams, Benin.** They use a large wooden bowl and long pestles (pounding sticks) to break up and mash the yams. These root crops are eaten at most meals. It is very hard work: much easier if it is shared! They are probably singing to help keep a rhythm for using the pestles. The baby will love this!

The southern part of West Africa, near the Equator, is forested. The tall trees are being felled for their hardwood. Many crops are grown in the forest area and sold overseas: cocoa (for chocolate-making); coffee, pineapples and bananas; rubber (for car and lorry tyres). The main food crops are root crops, such as cassava and yams.

Further north, the trees thin out and there is savanna. The tall grass with some trees is suitable for cattle farming. There are big herds of cattle, and beautiful leather goods are on sale in the markets. Cotton and groundnuts (peanuts) are grown in the savanna lands. The main food crops are grass-like: rice, maize and millet. In the far north of West Africa there is semi-desert: the Sahara is advancing southwards.

*Palm-oil harvest, Ghana.* These people are carrying heavy baskets full of oil-palm fruit. The oil palm grows in the hot, wet climate of the tropical forest. The fruits grow in bunches, with as many as 3000 bright-red palm fruits in a bunch. The fruit and the kernels are crushed in a factory to obtain oils. These oils are very useful for cooking and in making soap.

*Yeji ferry, Ghana.* This big ferry carries lorries, cars, people and their heavy loads across Lake Volta. This man-made lake flooded Ghana's main road to the north. As the water rose in the new lake, the trees and much of the wildlife died. A fifteenth of all Ghana's land was 'lost' under the lake, and new villages had to be built.

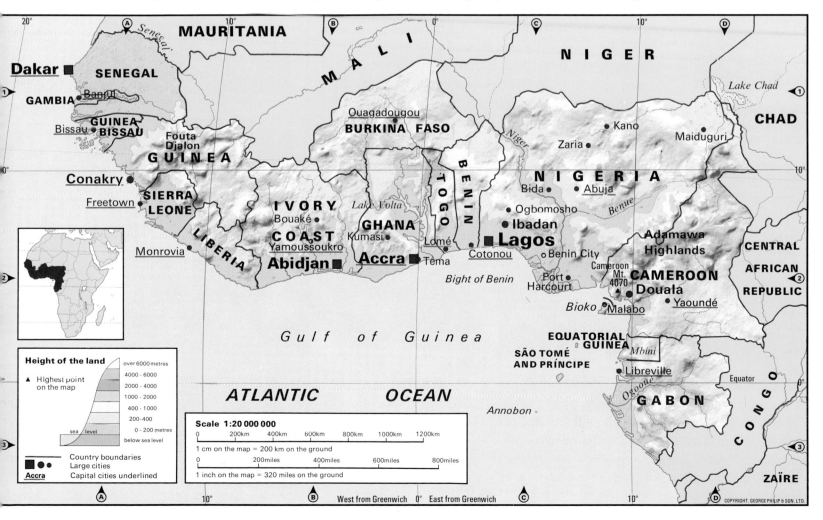

**Height of the land**

| | |
|---|---|
| over 6000 metres | |
| 4000 - 6000 | |
| 2000 - 4000 | |
| 1000 - 2000 | |
| 400 - 1000 | |
| 200 - 400 | |
| 0 - 200 metres | |
| below sea level | |

▲ Highest point on the map

sea level

■ ■ ● ● Country boundaries / Large cities
<u>Accra</u> Capital cities underlined

**Scale 1:20 000 000**

0  200km  400km  600km  800km  1000km  1200km
1 cm on the map = 200 km on the ground

0  200miles  400miles  600miles  800miles
1 inch on the map = 320 miles on the ground

West from Greenwich  0°  East from Greenwich

**57**

# CENTRAL AND EAST AFRICA

**AREA** 580,370 sq km
**POPULATION** 28,240,000
**MONEY** Kenya shilling

### ETHIOPIA

**AREA** 1,128,000 sq km
**POPULATION** 51,600,000
**MONEY** Birr

### ZAÏRE

**AREA** 2,344,885 sq km
**POPULATION** 44,504,000
**MONEY** Zaïre

Central Africa is mostly lowland, with magnificent trees in the tropical rainforest in Zaïre and Congo. Some timber is used for buildings and canoes (see photograph right); some is exported. The cleared land can grow many tropical crops.

East Africa is mostly high savanna land with long grass, and scattered trees. Some parts are reserved for wild animals; in other parts, there are large farms for export crops such as coffee and tea. But in most of East Africa, the people keep cattle and grow crops for their own needs.

The Somali Republic, Djibouti and Eritrea are desert areas, but the mountain areas of Ethiopia get plenty of rain. There have been terrible wars and famines in Ethiopia, Eritrea and Somalia.

In 1994 and 1995, a civil war in Rwanda led to a million deaths and more than a million refugees travelling to Zaïre and Tanzania. Wars like this damage people, the animals, and the environment (see below).

**The River Zaïre at Mbandaka.** Children who live near the river learn to paddle a dug-out canoe from an early age. The boats are hollowed out of a single tree with an axe. The River Zaïre is an important transport route. Mbandaka is a river port about four days by steamer from Kinshasa.

## MINERALS OF TANZANIA

Africa is mostly made of old, hard rocks. There are valuable minerals such as sapphires (top stamp) and diamonds (bottom stamp) in these rocks in some areas. They are cut and polished to become lovely gems. Despite its mineral wealth, Tanzania is one of the world's poorest countries.

**In a game reserve in Kenya,** a group of Grevy's Zebra graze the savanna grassland. In the dry season, the grass is brown, but in the rainy season it is tall and green. The game reserves are carefully managed and people come from all over the world to see the wildlife.

**Gorillas in Rwanda.** These gorillas live high up in the forested mountains. They are at risk because of the 1994–5 civil war.

**Buses in the centre of Nairobi, Kenya.** This modern capital city has many high-rise buildings – yet only 100 years ago there was no town here.

In all these countries, there is much poverty and people are moving to the cities. But there are many signs of development: new farm projects, new ports and roads, new clinics and schools.

The population of this area is growing fast. It has doubled in less than 25 years. Some of these countries have the world's highest population growth rates.

***Mount Kilimanjaro, Tanzania.*** *Africa's highest mountain is the beautiful cone of an old volcano. It is near the Equator, but high enough to have snow all year.*

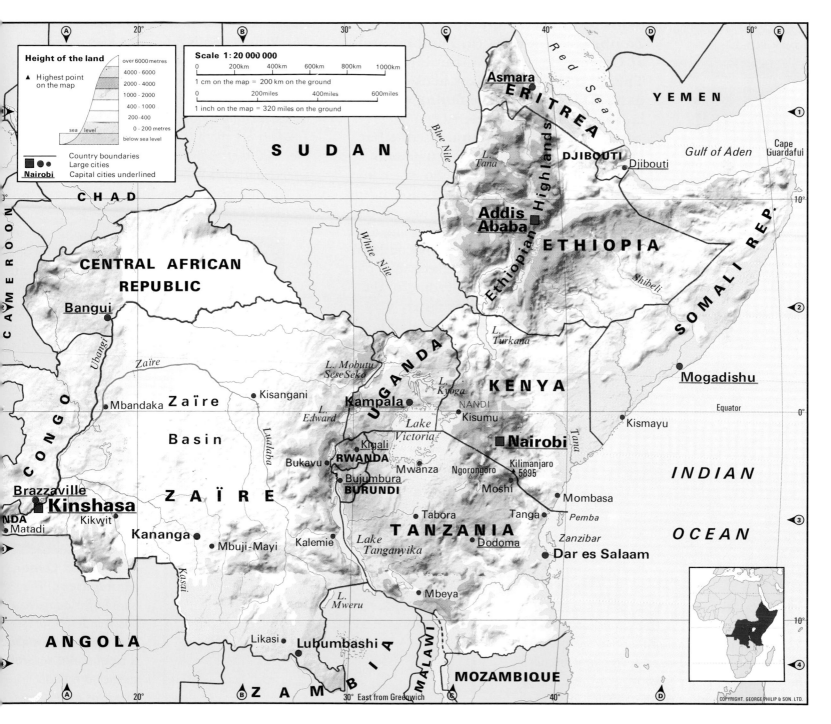

**Height of the land**

▲ Highest point on the map

over 6000 metres
4000 – 6000
2000 – 4000
1000 – 2000
400 – 1000
200 – 400
0 – 200 metres
sea level
below sea level

Country boundaries
Large cities
**Nairobi** Capital cities underlined

**Scale 1 : 20 000 000**

0   200km   400km   600km   800km   1000km

1 cm on the map = 200 km on the ground

0   200miles   400miles   600miles

1 inch on the map = 320 miles on the ground

# SOUTHERN AFRICA

## SOUTH AFRICA

**AREA** 1,219,916 sq km
**POPULATION** 44,000,000
**MONEY** Rand

## ANGOLA

**AREA** 1,246,700 sq km
**POPULATION** 10,844,000
**MONEY** Kwanza

## BOTSWANA

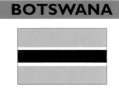

**AREA** 581,730 sq km
**POPULATION** 1,481,000
**MONEY** Pula

Most of southern Africa is a high, flat plateau. The rivers cannot be used by ships because of big waterfalls like the Victoria Falls (see photograph right). But the rivers can be useful. Two huge dams have been built on the River Zambezi – at Kariba (in Zambia) and at Cabora Bassa (in Mozambique). The map shows the lakes behind each dam. The power of the falling water is used to make electricity.

Angola and Mozambique used to be Portuguese colonies, and Portuguese is still their official language – though many different African languages are spoken, too. Most of the other countries shown on the map have English as their official language.

The map shows you that many southern African countries are landlocked: they have no coastline. The railways leading to the ports in neighbouring countries are very important. Copper from **Zambia** and **Botswana** is sent abroad in this way.

*The Victoria Falls* are on the River Zambezi, at the border of Zambia and Zimbabwe. Africans call the falls Mosi-oi-tunya – 'the smoke that thunders'. They were named after the English Queen Victoria by the explorer David Livingstone. The falls are more than a kilometre wide and over 100 metres high. The dense forest in the foreground relies on the spray from the falls.

## MOZAMBIQUE

**AREA** 801,590 sq km
**POPULATION** 17,800,000
**MONEY** Metical

*Cape Town, South Africa.* The flat-topped mountain is called 'Table Mountain'. It looks as flat as a table. When cloud covers it, it is called 'the tablecloth'! Cape Town is near the Cape of Good Hope, the most southerly point in Africa.

### A VILLAGE IN ZAMBIA

A Zambian girl drew this picture of her village during a lesson at her school. Her village is close to the River Zambezi in the west of Zambia. Look for a well, a man hoeing, a fisherman and a man looking after cattle. On the road there is a bus, a car and a van.

*Ring-tailed Lemur, Madagascar.* The island of Madagascar has wonderful forests and some of its wildlife is unique. But several species are under threat of extinction.

The **Republic of South Africa** is the wealthiest country in Africa. It has the richest gold mine in the world, and also the world's deepest mine. It is 3777 metres deep! South Africa was home to the world's largest diamond – found in 1905.

Most of the black people are still very poor. For many years, they were kept apart from the rich white people who used to rule the country. In 1994 they gained the vote and could share in their country's government.

**Namibia** and **Botswana** are dry areas, with small numbers of people. Some of the rivers in this area never reach the sea. The map on this page shows big swamps and 'salt pans': these are the places where the river water evaporates. **Lesotho** is a small mountainous country, completely surrounded by the Republic of South Africa.

**Madagascar** is the fourth largest island in the world. The people and their language are a mixture of African and Indonesian.

***Children in Mozambique*** *hope for a better future after many years of war. Their country is the poorest in Africa, and has also suffered from both disastrous floods and drought.*

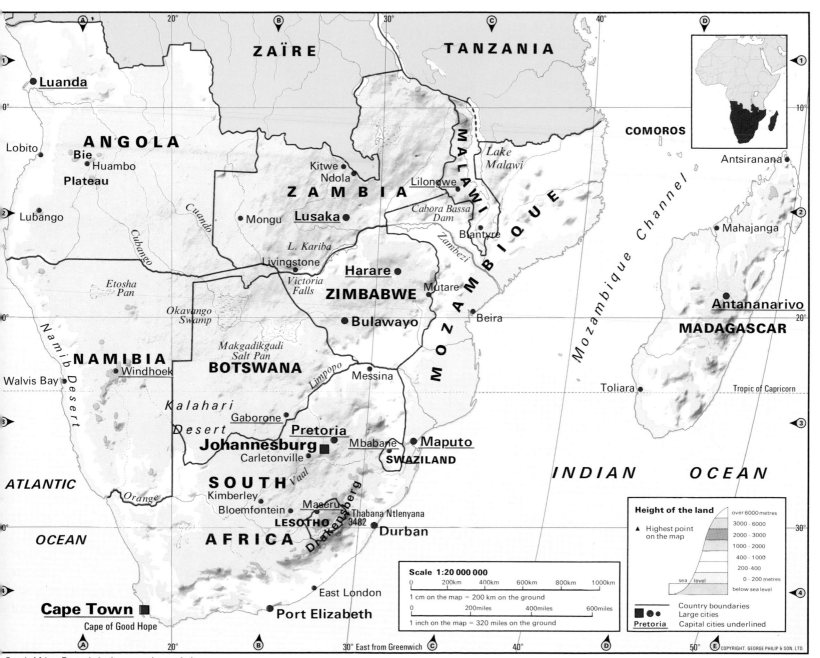

Scale 1:20 000 000

1 cm on the map = 200 km on the ground

1 inch on the map = 320 miles on the ground

**Height of the land**

| | |
|---|---|
| over 6000 metres | |
| 3000 - 6000 | |
| 2000 - 3000 | |
| 1000 - 2000 | |
| 400 - 1000 | |
| 200 - 400 | |
| 0 - 200 metres | |
| below sea level | |

▲ Highest point on the map

Country boundaries
Large cities
Pretoria   Capital cities underlined

South Africa, Pretoria is shown as the capital
ut the parliament meets in Cape Town.

**61**

# THE PACIFIC

This map shows half the world. Guess which place is furthest from a continent: it is to be found somewhere in the south Pacific. The Pacific Ocean also includes the deepest place in the world: the Mariana Trench (11,022 metres deep). It would take over an hour for a steel ball weighing half a kilogram to fall to the bottom!

There are thousands of islands in the Pacific. Some are volcanic mountains, while many others are low, flat coral islands. Coral also grows around the volcanoes.

A few islands have valuable minerals – for example Bougainville (copper) and Nauru (phosphates).

**Coral reef in French Polynesia,** *from the air. Coral BELOW sea level is ALIVE! A reef is built up from the shells of dead coral. Gradually plants colonize parts of the reef.*

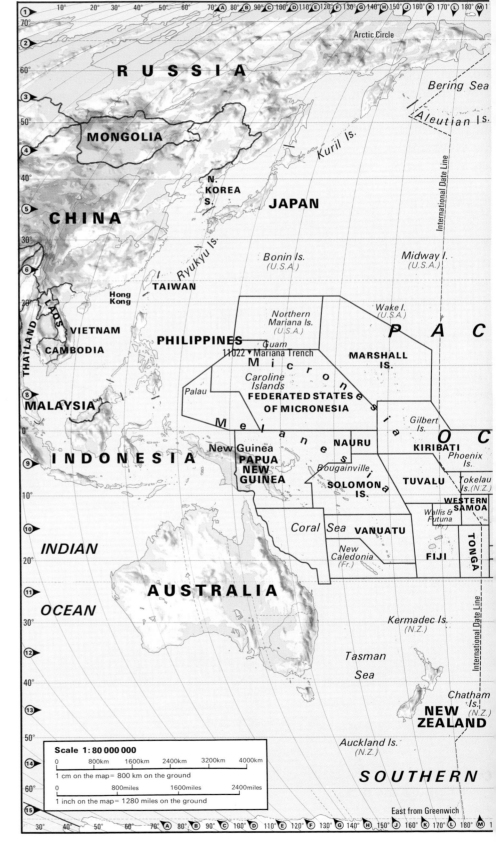

Most islanders are occupied in farming. Many tropical crops grow well; sugar-cane, bananas and pineapples are important exports.

Islands big enough for a full-sized airport, such as Fiji, the Samoan islands, Tahiti, and Hawaii (see page 72), now get many tourists.

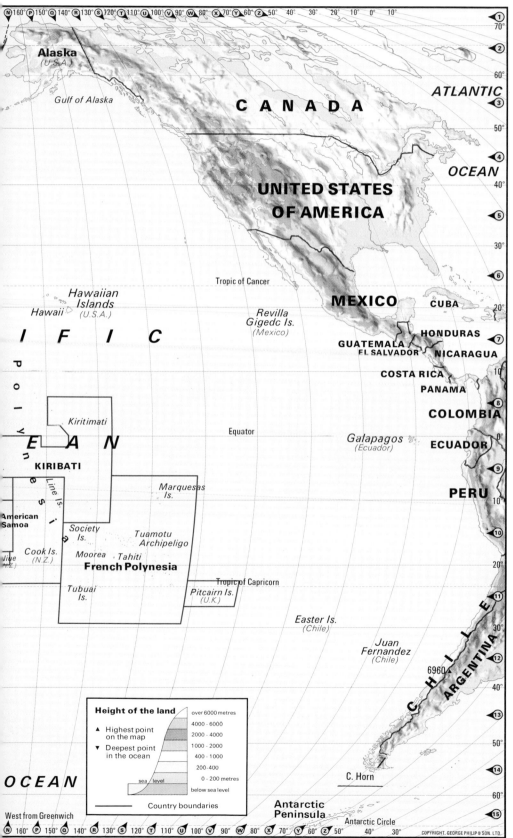

***Easter Island, South Pacific.*** *These huge stone sculptures each weigh about 50 tonnes! They were cut long ago with simple stone axes, and lifted with ropes and ramps — an amazing achievement for people who had no metal, no wheels and no machines. Look for Easter Island on the map (in square U11): it is one of the most remote places in the world. It is now owned by Chile, 3860 kilometres away in South America.*

## PACIFIC FACTS

**OCEAN AREA** 179,679,000 sq km – the world's biggest ocean

**HIGHEST POINT** Mount Wilhelm (Papua New Guinea), 4508 metres

**LOWEST POINT ON LAND** Lake Eyre (Australia), 16 metres below sea level

**DEEPEST PART OF OCEAN** Mariana Trench, 11,022 metres below surface. This is the deepest place on Earth.

**LONGEST RIVER** Murray–Darling (Australia), 3750 km

**LARGEST LAKE** Lake Eyre (Australia), 8900 sq km

**BIGGEST COUNTRY** Australia, 7,686,850 sq km

**SMALLEST COUNTRY** Nauru, 21 sq km

Most Pacific countries are large groups of small islands. Their boundaries are out at sea – just lines on a map. For example, Kiribati is 33 small coral atolls spread over 5,000,000 square kilometres of ocean.

# AUSTRALIA

## AUSTRALIA

**AREA** 7,686,850 sq km
**POPULATION** 18,107,000
**MONEY** Australian dollar

## THE GREAT BARRIER REEF

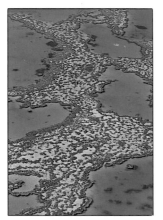

***The Great Barrier Reef** is the world's largest living thing! It is an area of coral over 2000 kilometres long, which grows in the warm sea near the coast of Queensland.*

*The reef is also home to colourful fish that swim among the coral. They can be seen from glass-bottomed boats.*

**A**ustralia is the world's largest island, but the world's smallest continent. It is the sixth-largest country in the world, smaller than the USA or Canada, but more than twice the size of India. Yet Australia has only about 18 million people. Most Australians are descended from people who came from Europe in the past 150 years.

Only a few people live in the mountains or in the outback – the enormous area of semi-desert and desert that makes up most of the country. The few outback people live on huge sheep and cattle farms, in mining towns, or on special reserves for the original Australians – the Aborigines.

***Ayers Rock** rises steeply out of the dry plains in central Australia. It is 348 metres high. The sides have deep gullies and strange caves. For the Aborigines, it is a holy place called Uluru. Many tourists come for the hard climb or to watch the rock glow deep red at sunset.*

***The Flying Doctor** can visit remote farms in the outback by air. The aeroplane is designed to be an ambulance, too. People in the outback use two-way radios to get medical advice, to call the doctor, and also to receive school lessons.*

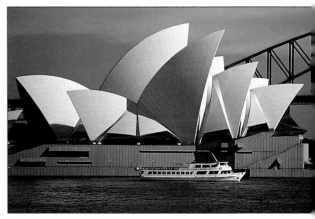

***Sydney Opera House** cost millions of dollars to build and has become the new symbol of Sydney. It is by the harbour, below the famous harbour bridge (in the background) which was built in Newcastle, UK!*

## AUSTRALIAN ANIMALS

**Australia** is not joined to any other continent. It has been a separate island for millions of years, and has developed its own unique wildlife. Most of the world's marsupials live in Australia.

The map shows that all the state capitals are on the coast. Canberra is a planned city built inland which became the national capital in 1927. Most Australians live near the coast and most live in towns. Even so, large areas of coast are almost uninhabited.

*TRICK QUESTION: Which was the biggest island in the world, before Australia was discovered? Think hard – then turn to page 96.

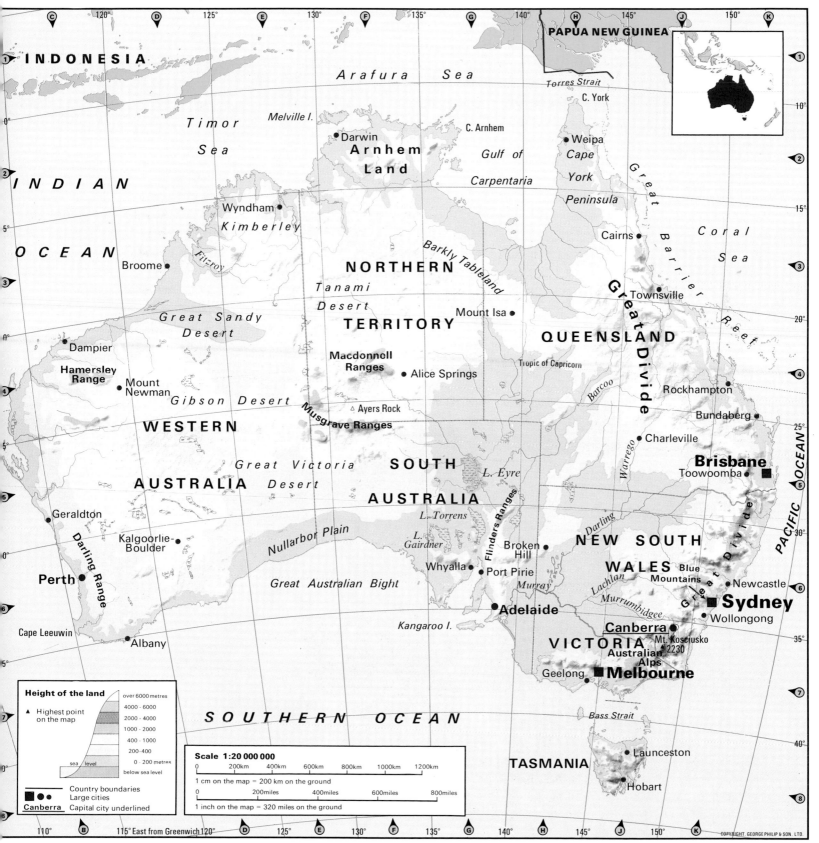

# NEW ZEALAND

## THE ANTIPODES

**New Zealand** is on the opposite side of the Earth from Europe. This 'double map' is printed as if you were looking right through a transparent globe. It shows that the far north of New Zealand is at the same latitude as North Africa, and that the far south of New Zealand is at the same latitude as the centre of France.

The two main islands that make up New Zealand are 2000 km east of Australia. Only 3½ million people live in the whole country. The capital is Wellington, near the centre of New Zealand, but the largest city is Auckland in the north.

The original inhabitants were the Maoris, but now they are only about 8 per cent of the population. Some place-names are Maori words, such as Rotorua, Whangarei and Wanganui.

South Island is the largest island, but has fewer people than North Island. There are more sheep than people! Mount Cook, the highest point in New Zealand (3753 metres) is in the spectacular Southern Alps. Tourists visit the far south to see the glaciers and fjords. The fast-flowing rivers are used for hydro-electricity.

**Auckland** is sometimes called 'the city of sails' because so many people own or sail a yacht here. The city centre (background) looks out over two huge natural harbours that are ideal for sailing. To the north is Waitemara Harbour and to the south is the shallow Manukau Harbour. Auckland is New Zealand's biggest city, and also an important port for huge container ships.

## NEW ZEALAND

**AREA** 268,680 sq km
**POPULATION** 3,567,000
**CURRENCY** Dollar

### KIWI FRUIT . . .

. . . **were known** as 'Chinese Gooseberries' until New Zealanders (nicknamed 'Kiwis') improved them, renamed them, and promoted them. Now they are a successful export crop for farmers, and many other countries also grow them – it is interesting to find out where YOUR kiwi fruit comes from.

**The Southern Alps** stretch the length of South Island. The fine scenery attracts tourists, and the grassland is used for sheep-grazing.

**The Maoris** lived in New Zealand before the Europeans came. Today, most live in North Island and many of their traditions have become part of New Zealand life. Perhaps you have seen the 'haka' on TV before an 'All Blacks' rugby game

North Island has a warmer climate than South Island. In some places you can see hot springs and boiling mud pools and there are also volcanoes. Fine trees and giant ferns grow in the forests, but much of the forest has been cleared for farming. Cattle are kept on the rich grasslands for meat and milk. Many different kinds of fruit grow well, including apples, kiwi fruit and pears, which are exported.

## GEOTHERMAL POWER

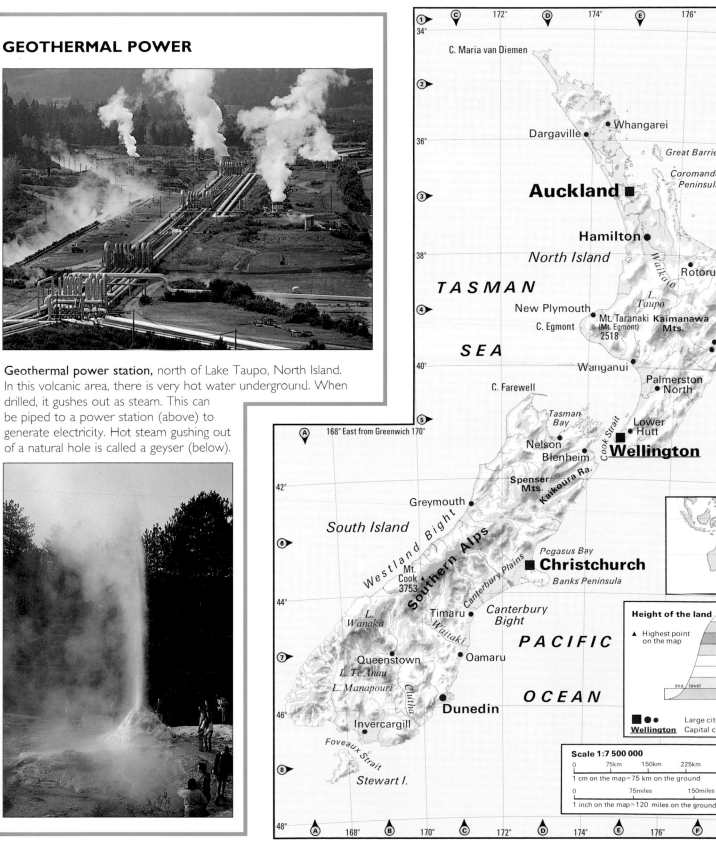

**Geothermal power station,** north of Lake Taupo, North Island. In this volcanic area, there is very hot water underground. When drilled, it gushes out as steam. This can be piped to a power station (above) to generate electricity. Hot steam gushing out of a natural hole is called a geyser (below).

### Map labels

C. Maria van Diemen
Dargaville
Whangarei
Great Barrier I.
Coromandel Peninsula
**Auckland**
**Hamilton**
Bay of Plenty
*North Island*
Waikato
Rotorua
**T A S M A N**
L. Taupo
Gisborne
New Plymouth
Mt. Taranaki (Mt. Egmont) 2518
Kaimanawa Mts.
C. Egmont
**S E A**
Napier
Hastings
Wanganui
Palmerston North
C. Farewell
Tasman Bay
Cook Strait
Lower Hutt
Nelson
**Wellington**
Blenheim
Spenser Mts.
Kaikoura Ra.
Greymouth
Westland Bight
*South Island*
Southern Alps
Pegasus Bay
**Christchurch**
Banks Peninsula
Mt. Cook 3753
Canterbury Plains
L. Wanaka
Timaru
Canterbury Bight
Waitaki
**P A C I F I C**
Queenstown
Oamaru
L. Te Anau
L. Manapouri
Clutha
**O C E A N**
**Dunedin**
Invercargill
Foveaux Strait
Stewart I.
168° East from Greenwich 170°

### Height of the land

| | |
|---|---|
| ▲ Highest point on the map | over 6000 metres |
| | 4000 - 6000 |
| | 2000 - 4000 |
| | 1000 - 2000 |
| | 400 - 1000 |
| | 200 - 400 |
| sea level | 0 - 200 metres |
| | below sea level |

■ ● ● Large cities
**Wellington** Capital city underlined

**Scale 1:7 500 000**

0   75km   150km   225km   300km   375km
1 cm on the map = 75 km on the ground

0   75miles   150miles   225miles
1 inch on the map = 120 miles on the ground

COPYRIGHT. GEORGE PHILIP & SON. LTD.

# NORTH AMERICA

**N**orth America includes many Arctic islands, a huge mainland area (quite narrow in Central America) and the islands in the Caribbean Sea. The map shows the great mountain ranges, including the Rockies, which are the most impressive feature of this continent.

Almost all of the west is high and mountainous, yet Death Valley is *below* sea level. The rocks have been folded into mountain ranges, but the highest peaks are volcanoes. The Appalachian Mountains in the east are also fold mountains. And the island chains of the north-west (the Aleutian Islands) and the south-east (the West Indies) are the tops of underwater ranges divided by shallow seas.

The political map of North America is quite a simple one. The boundary between Canada and the USA is mostly at exactly 49°N. Four of the five Great Lakes have one shore in Canada and one shore in the USA★. Canada's two biggest cities, Toronto and Montreal, are south of the 49° line! Find them on the map on page 71.

**Greenland** used to be a colony of Denmark, but now it is self-governing. Most of Greenland is covered by ice all year. See page 88 for more about Greenland.

★ Which ones? Answers on page 96.

*Flyovers, Los Angeles, USA. There are three levels of road at this road junction in Los Angeles; sometimes there are traffic jams as well! In 1994, a huge earthquake destroyed many road bridges.*

**Height of the land**

| |
| --- |
| over 6000 metres |
| 4000 - 6000 |
| 2000 - 4000 |
| 1000 - 2000 |
| 400 - 1000 |
| 200 - 400 |
| 0 - 200 metres |
| sea level |
| below sea level |

Deeper blue - deeper sea
▲ Highest point on the map

**Scale 1 : 50 000 000**

0    500km    1000km    1500km    2000km    2500km

1 cm on the map = 500 km on the ground

0    500miles    1000miles    1500miles

1 inch on the map = 800 miles on the ground

The eight countries of **Central America** have more complicated boundaries. Six of these countries have two coastlines. The map shows that one country has a coastline only on the Pacific Ocean, and one has a coastline only on the Caribbean Sea*. These countries are Spanish-speaking: in fact there are more Spanish speakers here than in Spain.

The **West Indies** are made up of islands; there are lots of countries too. One island has TWO countries on it*. They are shown in more detail on page 81. This area is often called 'The Caribbean'. Some West Indians have emigrated to the USA, Britain and France.

* Which ones? Answers on page 96.

**Market in St George's, Grenada.**
*The West Indies have hot sunshine and plenty of rain. This is an ideal climate for growing vegetables and fruit. These stalls are stacked high with local produce. Many islands have volcanic soil which is rich in minerals and very fertile.*

*Grenada is an island country which grows and exports bananas and nutmeg.*

### NORTH AMERICA FACTS

**AREA** 24,249,000 sq km
**HIGHEST POINT** Mount McKinley (Alaska), 6194 metres
**LOWEST POINT** Death Valley (California), 86 metres below sea level
**LONGEST RIVERS**
Red Rock–Missouri–Mississippi, 5970 km
Mackenzie–Peace, 4240 km
**LARGEST LAKE** Lake Superior*, 82,350 sq km
**BIGGEST COUNTRY**
Canada, 9,976,140 sq km
**SMALLEST COUNTRY** Grenada (West Indies), 344 sq km
**RICHEST COUNTRY** USA
**POOREST COUNTRY** Haiti
**MOST CROWDED COUNTRY** Barbados
**LEAST CROWDED COUNTRY** Canada

* The world's largest freshwater lake

# CANADA

## CANADA

**AREA** 9,976,140 sq km
**POPULATION** 29,972,000
**MONEY** Canadian dollar
**CAPITAL** Ottawa
**NATIONAL DAY** 1 July

## STAMPS

*This stamp is an air-picture of the prairies of central Canada. The huge flat fields of grain reach to the far horizon, and beyond.*

*In western Canada, the Rocky Mountains are high and jagged. There are glaciers among the peaks. The Rockies stretch for 4800 km through both Canada and the USA. They were a great barrier to the early explorers and to the early settlers and railway engineers.*

**O**nly one country in the world is bigger than Canada★, but 30 countries have more people than Canada. Most of Canada is almost empty: very few people live on the islands of the north, or in the Northwest Territories, or in the western mountains, or near Hudson Bay. The farmland of the prairies (see the top stamp) is uncrowded too. So . . . where do Canadians live?

The answer is that more Canadians live in cities than in the countryside. The map shows where the biggest cities are – all of them are in the southern part of Canada, and none are as far north as Norway or Sweden in Europe.

These photographs show Canada in summer. In winter, it is very cold indeed in both central and northern Canada. Children go to school even when it is 40° below zero. The mildest winters are in the south-west, around Vancouver.

★ Which country? See page 9.

**Quebec City.** *The Chateau Frontenac (seen on the left) is built in the style of a French chateau (castle). This part of Canada was once owned by the French, and the people still speak French. On the right is the port beside the River St Lawrence. Large ocean-going ships can dock here.*

**The Niagara Falls** *are between Lake Erie and Lake Ontario, on the border of the USA (in the distance) and Canada. One part is called the Horseshoe Falls: can you see why? Ships have to use a canal with locks to get past the falls. The falling water is used to generate hydro-electricity.*

**A long-distance train** *travels through a pass in the Rocky Mountains. The trans-Canada railway helped unite Canada as one country 110 years ago.*

## LANGUAGES IN CANADA

Canada has two official languages: French and English. So Canadian stamps say 'Postes/Postage', instead of only 'Postage'. Most of the French-speaking Canadians live in the province of Quebec.

The biggest city in Quebec is Montreal: it is four times as big as Ottawa, the capital of Canada.

**Vancouver, British Columbia:** *the biggest city in the west of Canada.*

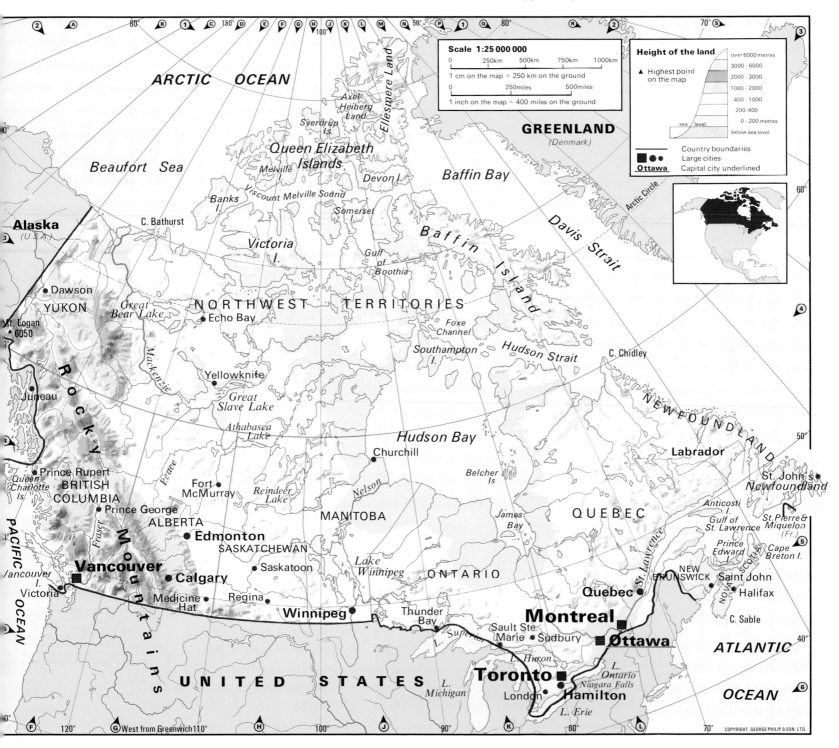

Scale 1:25 000 000

1 cm on the map = 250 km on the ground

1 inch on the map = 400 miles on the ground

Height of the land

over 6000 metres
3000 - 6000
2000 - 3000
1000 - 2000
400 - 1000
200 - 400
0 - 200 metres
below sea level

▲ Highest point on the map

sea level

Country boundaries
Large cities
**Ottawa** Capital city underlined

ARCTIC OCEAN

Axel Heiberg Land

Ellesmere Land

Sverdrup Is.

GREENLAND
(Denmark)

Beaufort Sea

Queen Elizabeth Islands

Melville I.

Devon I.

Baffin Bay

Banks I.

Viscount Melville Sound

Somerset I.

Victoria I.

Gulf of Boothia

Baffin Island

Davis Strait

C. Bathurst

Arctic Circle

Alaska
(U.S.A.)

Dawson

YUKON

Mt. Logan
▲ 6050

Great Bear Lake

NORTHWEST TERRITORIES

Echo Bay

Foxe Channel

Southampton I.

Hudson Strait

C. Chidley

Juneau

Mackenzie

Yellowknife

Great Slave Lake

NEWFOUNDLAND

R O C K Y

Athabasca Lake

Hudson Bay

Churchill

Labrador

Prince Rupert

Queen Charlotte Is.

BRITISH COLUMBIA

Pearce

Fort McMurray

Reindeer Lake

Nelson

Belcher Is.

James Bay

QUEBEC

St. John's
Newfoundland

Anticosti I.
Gulf of
St. Lawrence

St. Pierre & Miquelon
(Fr.)

Prince George

ALBERTA

Edmonton

SASKATCHEWAN

Lake Winnipeg

ONTARIO

Prince Edward I.

Cape Breton I.

Vancouver I.

Vancouver

Fraser

Calgary

Saskatoon

St. Lawrence

NEW BRUNSWICK

Saint John

Victoria

Medicine Hat

Regina

Winnipeg

Thunder Bay

Quebec

Halifax

C. Sable

Montreal

Ottawa

PACIFIC OCEAN

M o u n t a i n s

L. Superior

Sault Ste. Marie

Sudbury

ATLANTIC

UNITED STATES

L. Michigan

Toronto

L. Huron

L. Ontario

Niagara Falls

London

Hamilton

OCEAN

L. Erie

West from Greenwich

COPYRIGHT. GEORGE PHILIP & SON. LTD.

# USA

**W**ho are 'the Americans'? Of every 100 people in the USA, over 80 have ancestors from Europe. The first colonists came from Britain, France and Spain, but later on, people came from almost all parts of Europe to the USA.

About 12 people out of every 100 came from West Africa, brought to the USA as slaves to work in the southern states. By 1865, the slaves were free. Many black Americans now live in the north-east. More recently, many Spanish-speaking people have arrived from Mexico and Puerto Rico.

There are now fewer than one million American Indians in the USA, some of whom live on special reservations.

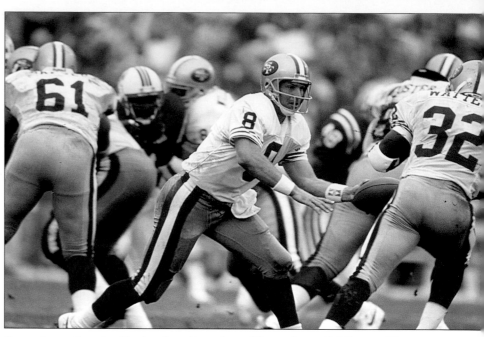

**American football:** the San Francisco 49ers, from California. The teams often have to travel many thousands of kilometres for each game. The players travel by air – it takes three days to cross the USA by train!

## STARS AND STRIPES

United States 13c

*In 1776 there were only 13 states in the USA: so the US flag had 13 stars and 13 stripes. As more and more states joined*

USA 15c

*the USA, more stars were added to the flag. Now there are 50 states, and 50 stars.*

### HAWAII

**Hawaii**

*is the newest state in the USA: it became a state in 1959. The picture shows Waikiki beach in Honolulu, the biggest city. Honolulu is on Oahu island. These faraway Pacific islands are the tops of volcanoes, over 3000 km from mainland USA (see map page 63). If the height of Mauna Kea is measured from the seabed, it is 10,023 metres: the world's highest mountain. The islands are the most southerly part of the USA.*

## STAMP

First Moon Landing, 1969

**An American** was the first man on the Moon. The astronaut is holding the USA flag. Above his head is the Earth, half in darkness.

## USA

**AREA** 9,372,610 sq km
**POPULATION** 263,563,000
**MONEY** US dollar
**CAPITAL** Washington, DC

The map shows the 50 states of the USA. The first 13 states were on the east coast, settled by Europeans who had sailed across the Atlantic. As the Americans moved westwards, so more and more states were formed. The western states are bigger than the states in the east. You can see their straight boundaries on the map.

## DISTANCE CHART

Read the chart just like a tables-chart, or a graph. The distance chart shows how big the USA is. How far is it from Seattle to Miami? Or from New Orleans to Chicago? (Answers on page 96.)

| Road distances in km | New York | Miami | Chicago | New Orleans | Seattle |
|---|---|---|---|---|---|
| Miami | 2138 | | | | |
| Chicago | 1346 | 2198 | | | |
| New Orleans | 2131 | 1406 | 1488 | | |
| Seattle | 4613 | 5445 | 3288 | 4211 | |
| San Francisco | 4850 | 4915 | 3499 | 3622 | 1352 |

## ALASKA

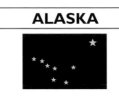

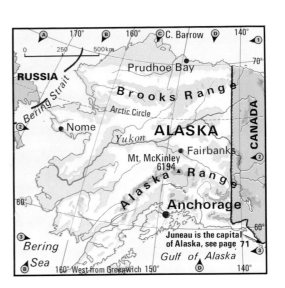

*Alaska* is the biggest state of the USA – but it has the fewest people. It was bought from Russia in 1867 for $7 million: the best bargain ever, particularly as oil was discovered a hundred years later. Oil has helped Alaska to become rich. Timber and fish are the other main products. Much of Alaska is mountainous or covered in forest. In the north, there is darkness all day in December, and months of ice-cold weather. But in the short summer, visitors love the long days and short nights. Farming is not possible in most of Alaska – except in the far south.

These are 48 of the 50 states.
The other two are Alaska (map above) and Hawaii (map opposite)
★ State capital

ABBREVIATIONS
VT. = Vermont
N.H. = New Hampshire
MASS. = Massachusetts
CONN. = Connecticut
D.C. = District of Columbia

COPYRIGHT. GEORGE PHILIP & SON. LTD.

# EASTERN USA

**OHIO**

**MARYLAND**

***Washington, DC, is the capital city.*** *The tall pillar is a monument to George Washington, who became the first President of the USA in 1776. The city is named after him. The building with the tall dome is the Capitol.*

The map shows only half the USA, but over three-quarters of the population live in this half of the country.

The great cities of the north-east were the first big industrial areas in America. Pittsburgh's American football team is still called the Pittsburgh Steelers, even though many of the steelworks have closed down.

In recent years, many people have moved from the 'snow-belt' of the north to the 'sun-belt' of the south. New industries are booming in the south, where once there was much poverty. And many older people retire to Florida, where even midwinter feels almost like summer.

In the south of the USA it is hot enough for cotton, tobacco and peanuts to be successful crops. The palm tree on the flag of South Carolina (below, right) suggests that the climate of this part of America is nearly tropical.

The Appalachian Mountains are beautiful, especially in the fall (autumn), when the leaves of the trees turn red. But this area is the poorest part of the USA. Coal mines have closed and farmland is poor. The good farmland is west of the Appalachians, where you can drive for hundreds of kilometres past wheat and sweetcorn.

***Canterbury Church, New Hampshire.***
*The north-east corner of the USA is called New England and was settled by English colonists. This church by the village green is very like old England! The settlers named their towns and villages after places they had known in England.*

## WHICH US CITY IS MOST IMPORTANT?

Washington, DC, is the capital city, where the President lives. But New York has far more people and industries than Washington. So *both* are the most important city – but in different ways.

***Manhattan Island, New York.*** *The world's first skyscrapers were built on Manhattan Island: the hard granite rock gave good foundations. The older skyscrapers each have a different shape; the newer ones are flat-topped.*

**TENNESSEE**

**S. CAROLINA**

**FLORIDA**

Every US state has its own flag: six state flags are on the page opposite. Several states were named after kings and queens of England – in the days when these states were English colonies. For example, CAROLina (North and South) use the Latin name for King Charles I; MARYland is named after his wife, Queen Mary, and GEORGia is named after King George II. But LOUISiana is named after King Louis XIV of France because France colonized the Mississippi.

## GREAT LAKES

Try using the first letters of the Great Lakes to make a sentence:

| | |
|---|---|
| **S**uperior | **S**uper |
| **M**ichigan | **M**an |
| **H**uron | **H**elps |
| **E**rie | **E**very |
| **O**ntario | **O**ne |

Now you'll *never* forget the west-to-east order of the Great Lakes!

## THE MISSISSIPPI

The Mississippi River was known as the 'Great River Road' because it was an important route into the heart of the USA. 'Stern-wheeler' paddle-steamers travelled the river with cargoes. It is still an important river today. Dams (above) and locks make it easier for big barges to use the river. The dams also help to reduce the risk of floods.

GREAT RIVER ROAD

***Oak Alley Plantation, Louisiana.***
*The cotton planters in the south lived in fine mansions like this one. Their wealth was based on slavery. The slaves lived in very different homes. No wonder the slaves wanted to be free! In 1865, slavery was abolished in the USA.*

# WESTERN USA

**COLORADO**

**SOUTH DAKOTA**

Many parts of the western USA have hardly any people. The Rocky Mountains are beautiful for holidays, but it is hard to make a living there.

The only big city on the high plateaus west of the Rockies is Salt Lake City, Utah. Some former mining towns are now 'ghost towns': when the mines closed, all the people left. The toughest area of all is the desert land of Arizona in the south-west. The mountains and deserts were a great problem to the pioneers, but today the spectacular scenery and wildlife is preserved in large national parks.

*The 'Wild West'.* Scenes like this one are rare now, except when they are put on for the many tourists who visit the area. But in the days of the 'Wild West', 100 years or more ago, the skills of cowboys were vital. Look carefully – this picture shows a cowgirl rounding up horses!

*Wheat harvest, USA.* A huge combine harvester moves across a field of wheat. Up to 150 years ago, this land was covered in grass and grazed by buffaloes. Much of this wheat will go abroad.

## WHAT DO THE NAMES MEAN?

The Spanish were the first settlers in the western USA, and they have left us many Spanish names. Can you match the name and its meaning? (Answers on page 96.)

| | |
|---|---|
| **Amarillo** (Texas) | The pass |
| **Colorado** | Yellow |
| **El Paso** (Texas) | The angels |
| **Los Angeles** | St Francis |
| **San José** | Coloured |
| **San Francisco** | St Joseph |

*Energy conservation.* A great idea! Americans use more energy than anyone else.

**WYOMING**

**ARIZONA**

**NEW MEXICO**

*Grand Canyon, Arizona.* The Colorado River has cut a huge canyon 1½ kilometres deep and several kilometres wide in this desert area of the USA. The mountains slowly rose, while the river kept carving a deeper valley.

**NEBRASKA**

**OKLAHOMA**

**TEXAS**

The Great Plains east of the Rocky Mountains are flat but high. Denver has the 'Mile-high Stadium'! These dry plains have enormous cattle ranches. Where there is enough rain, crops of wheat and sweetcorn (maize) stretch to the horizon.

The Pacific coastlands of the north-west have plenty of rain and the climate is quite like north-west Europe. The mountains and valleys are thickly forested and timber is an important product.

## CALIFORNIA

California now has more people in it than any other state. It has many advantages. In the Central Valley, the climate is right for many crops: oranges from California are well known, and grapes grow well and are made into wine. The desert of the south is attractive to retired people – many people migrate here from all over the USA.

**A street-car in San Francisco.**
Street-cars still climb the steep hills in San Francisco, California. A moving cable runs beneath the street. The car is fixed to the cable and starts with a jerk! In the background you can see an inlet of the Pacific and Alcatraz – once a top-security prison island.

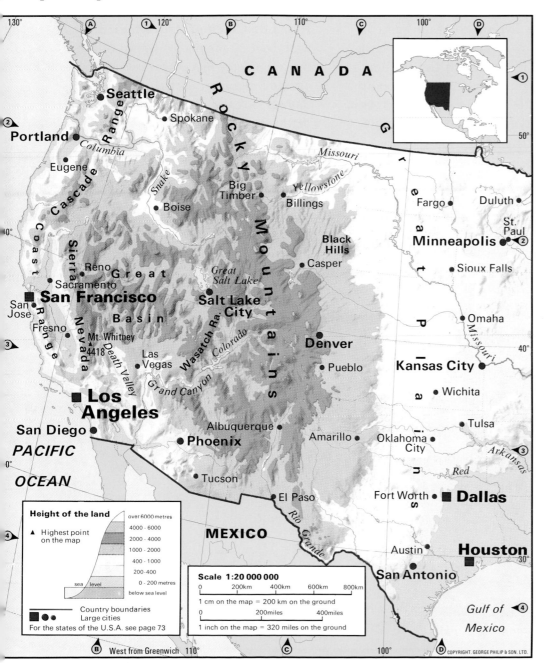

**Height of the land**

▲ Highest point on the map

| | |
|---|---|
| over 6000 metres | |
| 4000 - 6000 | |
| 2000 - 4000 | |
| 1000 - 2000 | |
| 400 - 1000 | |
| 200-400 | |
| 0 - 200 metres | |
| sea level | |
| below sea level | |

Country boundaries
Large cities
For the states of the U.S.A. see page 73

**Scale 1:20 000 000**
0    200km    400km    600km    800km
1 cm on the map = 200 km on the ground
0    200miles    400miles
1 inch on the map = 320 miles on the ground

COPYRIGHT. GEORGE PHILIP & SON. LTD.

West from Greenwich

**Hollywood** is a suburb of Los Angeles. Rich film-stars live here in expensive houses. The clear blue skies and lack of rain were helpful to film-makers. But now, Los Angeles has so many cars there is more smog from pollution than clear skies.

**77**

# CENTRAL AMERICA

## MEXICO

**AREA** 1,958,200 sq km
**POPULATION** 93,342,000
**MONEY** New peso

## PANAMA

**AREA** 77,080 sq km
**POPULATION** 2,629,000
**MONEY** Balboa

## GUATEMALA

**AREA** 108,890 sq km
**POPULATION** 10,624,000
**MONEY** Quetzal

**M**exico is by far the most important country on this map. Over 91 million people live in Mexico – more than in any country in Europe. Mexico City has a population of about 19 million: it is one of the biggest cities in the world. A major earthquake did much damage there in 1985.

Most Mexicans live on the high plateau of central Mexico. Industries are growing fast in Mexico City and near the border with the USA. There are very few people in the northern desert, in Lower California in the north-west, in the southern jungle, or in Yucatan in the east.

The other seven countries on this map are quite small. None of them has as many people as Mexico City!

Once ruled by Spain, these countries have been independent since the 1820s. Civil wars have caused many problems in Central America. But the climate is good for growing many tropical crops.

**Ruins at Chichen Itza, Mexico.** *Great temples were built by the people known as Mayas over a thousand years ago. These amazing ruins are in Yucatan, the most easterly part of Mexico. The tourists look tiny, which shows you how HUGE the pyramid is. Today, this is an area of jungle.*

## BELIZE

**AREA** 22,960 sq km
**POPULATION** 216,000
**MONEY** Belize dollar

## TORTILLAS – A RECIPE FOR YOU TO COOK

**Ingredients**
225 grams of maize flour (sweetcorn flour)
salt and water

**Method**
**1** Mix the maize flour, salt and water into a soft dough.
**2** Pat into round shapes about ½ centimetre thick, and 12 centimetres across.
**3** Melt a little margarine in a frying-pan.
**4** Place the tortillas in the hot frying-pan.
**5** For best results, turn the tortillas over.
**6** Serve at once!

You have now cooked one of the most important meals of Central America. Maize (sweetcorn) was developed as a crop in the Americas, and is now grown in many parts of the world. You eat maize often as Corn Flakes and semolina.

**The Toucan** *is sometimes called the 'banana-beak bird', for an obvious reason! It eats fruit and lives in the forest, nesting in a hole in a tree. If the forest is cleared, it will have nowhere to live.*

# THE PANAMA CANAL

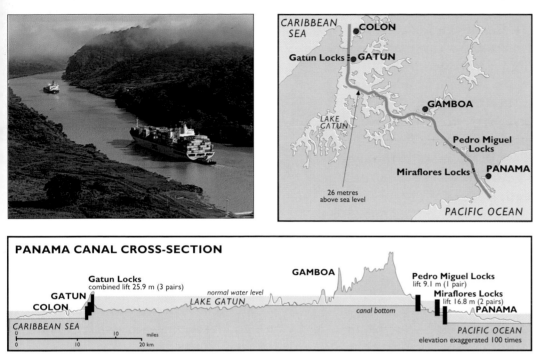

## PANAMA CANAL CROSS-SECTION

**The Panama Canal** links the Caribbean Sea with the Pacific Ocean. It was opened in 1914. Many workers died of fever while digging the canal through the jungle. It is 82 km long, and the deepest cutting is 82 metres deep – the world's biggest 'ditch'!

There are six locks along the route of the canal. The photograph (left) shows two ships travelling through the canal. The map and diagram show that part of the route is through Lake Gatun, at 26 metres above sea level. So the ships have to pass through three locks at each end.

Over 15,000 ships use the canal each year, and sometimes there are 'traffic jams' at the locks: it is the busiest big-ship canal in the world. Before the Panama Canal was built, the only sea route from the Pacific to the Atlantic was round South America.

In which direction are ships travelling from the Caribbean to the Pacific? Does this surprise you? Look at the map below.

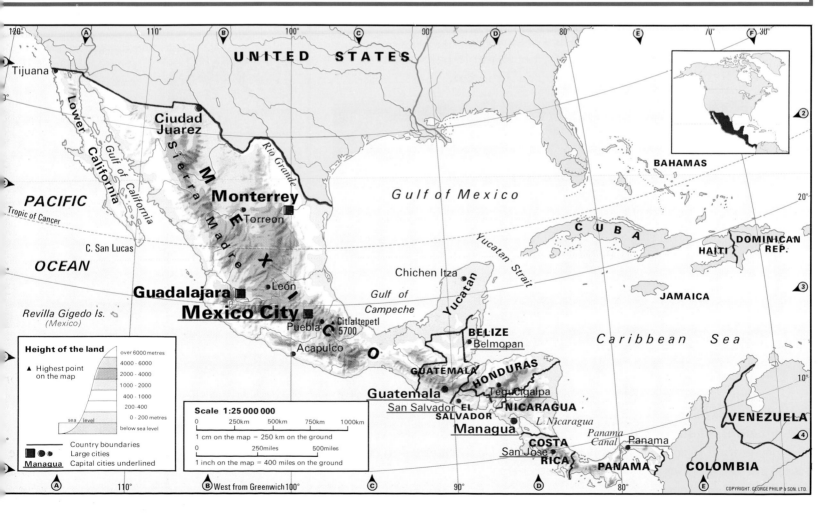

# WEST INDIES

### JAMAICA

**AREA** 10,990 sq km
**POPULATION** 2,700,000
**MONEY** Jamaican dollar

### CUBA

**AREA** 110,860 sq km
**POPULATION** 11,050,000
**MONEY** Cuban peso

### HAITI

**AREA** 27,750 sq km
**POPULATION** 7,180,000
**MONEY** Gourde

**T**he West Indies are a large group of islands in the Caribbean Sea. Some islands are high and volcanic, others are low coral islands – but all of them are beautiful. Most West Indians have African ancestors: they were brought from West Africa as slaves, to work in the sugar and tobacco fields. And in Trinidad, workers came from India as well.

Most of the islands are now independent countries – and tourism is more important than farming in many places. Winter is the best time to visit; summer is very hot and humid, with the risk of hurricanes. In recent years, many West Indians have emigrated to the UK from Commonwealth islands, to France from Guadeloupe and Martinique, and to the USA from Puerto Rico. The most important crops for export are bananas and other fruit, sugar and tobacco. A few islands have developed their minerals, for example bauxite in Jamaica and oil in Trinidad.

***Coconut palms and beach, Barbados.***
*It is beautiful – but beware! The tropical sun can quickly burn your skin. And if you seek shade under the coconut palms, you might get hit by a big coconut! Even so, the West Indies are very popular with tourists – especially Americans escaping from cold winters.*

## TOURISM – GOOD & BAD NEWS

Tourism is GOOD news because it brings money and jobs to many West Indian islands. The sunny weather means tourists come all year round. There is work in the hotels and restaurants. Farmers can sell more vegetables and a great variety of delicious fruit (right). Beautiful scenery is looked after so that tourists will come and visit – waterfalls, hot springs, old forts and churches as well as coral reefs and lovely beaches. But tourism can also be BAD news . . .

pollution; noise; waste of water; and many local people do not want to be stared at and photographed by rich tourists who may not treat them as equals.

***Dutch colonial houses, Curaçao.*** *The island of Curaçao has been Dutch for many years. The colonists came from the Netherlands, and tried to build houses just like the ones at home. Several other small West Indian islands still have European connections.*

**The flag of Jamaica** (far left) has a meaning: GOLD stands for sunshine and natural resources; GREEN for farming and future hope; BLACK for hardships, past and present.

The West Indies used to be colonies of European countries. Today, most of the islands are independent, but still have close links with Europe. Look at the map; can you spot★:

● An island that is part of France?
● An island that is owned by the Netherlands?
● An island owned by the UK?
● A group of islands – half are owned by the UK; half by the USA?

★ Answers on page 96.)

**Beware of the hurricane season!**
*What a contrast to the peaceful beach (see picture, left)! Violent tropical storms are a danger every summer. Strong winds can reach over 300 kilometres per hour, with torrential rain. They uproot trees and wreck boats and buildings; floods damage crops.*

**Loading bananas, Dominica.** *Bananas are the main export of several islands. Here women are carrying heavy loads of bananas on their heads to the small boats which take the bananas to the Geest banana ship. The bananas travel to Europe in this refrigerated ship. Loading the ship is easier in deep-water harbours.*

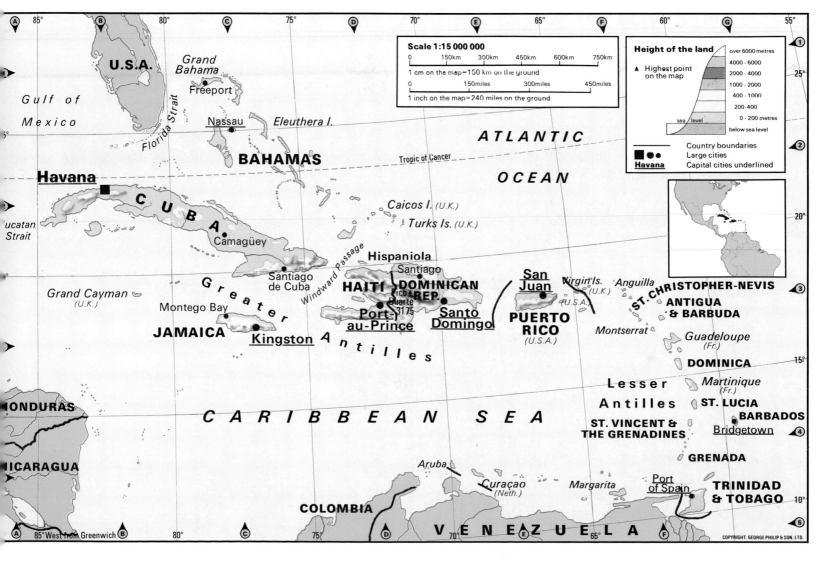

# SOUTH AMERICA

**A** tour of South America would be very exciting. At the Equator are the hot steamy jungles of the Amazon lowlands. To the west comes the great climb up to the Andes Mountains. The peaks are so high that even the volcanoes are snow-capped all year. Travellers on buses and trains are offered extra oxygen to breathe, because the air is so thin.

Squeezed between the Andes and the Pacific Ocean in Peru and northern Chile is the world's driest desert – the Atacama Desert, which stretches southwards from the border with Peru for nearly 1600 kilometres.

Further south in Chile are more wet forests – but these forests are cool. The monkey-puzzle tree originates here. But eastwards, in Argentina, there is less rain and more grass. Cattle on the Pampas are rounded up by cowboys, and further south is the very cold and dry area called Patagonia where sheep farming is important.

***Reed boats on Lake Titicaca,*** *the highest navigable lake in the world. It is high in the Andes, at 3811 metres above sea level. Totora reeds grow around the shores, and the Indians tie bundles of reeds together to make fishing boats. The picture shows the reed shelters they use while they make the boats and go fishing. In the background you can see a mountain rising from the plateau.*

*Lake Titicaca is shared between Peru and Bolivia. A steam-powered ferry boat travels the length of the lake.*

*Why is Lake Titicaca the only stretch of water available for the Bolivian navy? (Check the map!)*

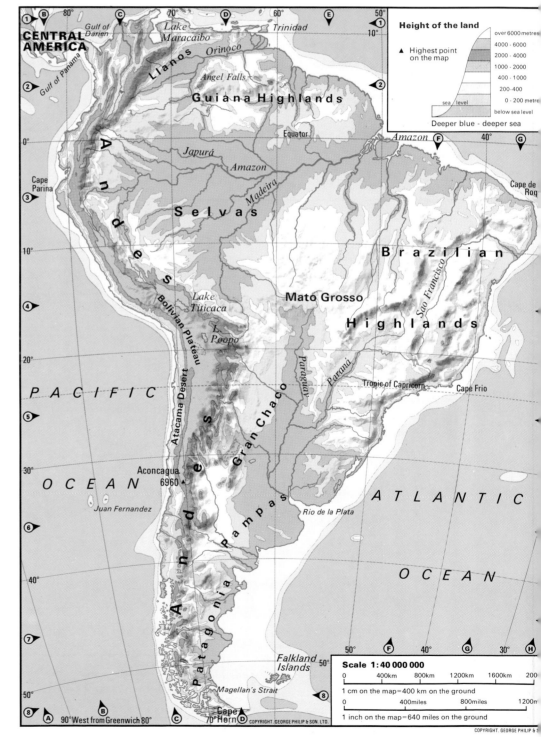

**82**

South America stretches further south than any other continent (apart from Antarctica). The cold and stormy tip of South America, Cape Horn, is only 1000 kilometres from Antarctica.

In every South American country, the population is growing fast. Most of the farmland is owned by a few rich people, and many people are desperately poor. Young people are leaving the countryside for the cities, most of which are encircled by shanty towns. There is rapid progress in the big cities, but many people do not benefit.

ONE country occupies nearly half the total area of South America, and has over half the population of the whole continent: BRAZIL.

**Brasília, Brazil.** *Brasília became the new capital of Brazil in 1960. It is a planned town, with tall office blocks and large open spaces. This is fine for car owners, but not for others as there are very few trees although the weather is very hot. Most Brazilians live near the coast, and Brasília was a brave attempt to get people to move inland. Over a million people now live there.*

## SOUTH AMERICA FACTS

**AREA** 17,600,000 sq km

**HIGHEST POINT** Mount Aconcagua (Argentina), 6960 metres

**LOWEST POINT** No land below sea level

**LONGEST RIVER** Amazon, 6448 km

**LARGEST LAKE** Lake Titicaca (Bolivia and Peru), 8285 sq km

**BIGGEST COUNTRY** Brazil, 8,511,970 sq km

**SMALLEST COUNTRY** Surinam*, 163,270 sq km

**RICHEST COUNTRY** Venezuela

**POOREST COUNTRY** Guyana

**MOST CROWDED COUNTRY** Ecuador

**LEAST CROWDED COUNTRY** Surinam

**HIGHEST WATERFALL** Angel Falls, 979 metres (a world record)

* French Guiana is smaller, but it is not independent

# TROPICAL SOUTH AMERICA

## BRAZIL

**AREA** 8,511,970 sq km
**POPULATION** 161,416,000
**MONEY** Cruzeiro real

## PERU

**AREA** 1,285,220 sq km
**POPULATION** 23,588,000
**MONEY** Sol

## COLOMBIA

**AREA** 1,138,910 sq km
**POPULATION** 34,948,000
**MONEY** Peso

**B**razil is by far the biggest country in South America, and has more people (about 161 million) than the rest of South America put together.

Most people still live near the coast. Parts of the Amazon forest are now being settled, but large areas inland are still almost empty. The poorest parts are in the north-east, where the rains often fail, and in the shanty towns around the cities. Modern industry is growing very fast, but there are still too few jobs. Brazil has pioneered fuel made from sugar-cane for cars and trucks.

Colombia, Ecuador, Peru and Bolivia are known as the Andean states. Colombia is known for its coffee. Bananas and other tropical crops grow near the coast of Ecuador, but the capital city is high in the mountains. Peru relies on mountain rivers to bring water to the dry coastal area. Bolivia has the highest capital city in the world. It is the poorest country in South America: farming is difficult and even the tin mines hardly make a profit.

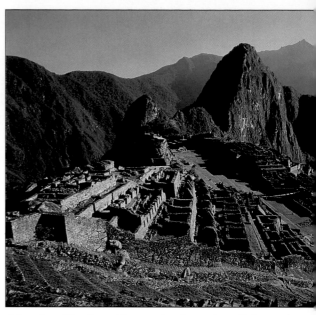

*Machu Picchu, Peru,* the lost city of the Incas, is perched on a mountainside 2400 metres above sea level. The last Inca emperor probably lived here in 1580. The ruins were rediscovered in 1911.

## ECUADOR

**AREA** 283,560 sq km
**POPULATION** 11,384,000
**MONEY** Sucre

*Going to market, Peru.* This lady is a descendant of the Incas who lived in Peru before the Spanish arrived. She carries her baby on her back in a fine woven blanket. In most South American countries, the Indians are among the poorest people.

*Amazon jungle.* The hot, wet jungle covers thousands of kilometres. There is no cool season, and the forest is always green. The trees can be 50 metres high. New roads and villages, mines and dams are being built in the Brazilian jungle, and parts of the forest are being destroyed.

### THE GALAPAGOS ISLANDS

These volcanic islands belong to Ecuador but are 1000 kilometres from the mainland. They have unique plants and animals because they have been isolated for so long. The giant tortoises are the most famous and spectacular 'residents'.

Venezuela is the richest country in South America because of its mineral wealth. Oil is pumped up from beneath Lake Maracaibo, and iron ore is mined from the plateau south of the River Orinoco. The world's highest waterfall, the Angel Falls, is in Venezuela.

In Guyana there are important deposits of bauxite, which is used to make aluminium. Guyana was once British and Surinam was once Dutch. But French Guiana is *still* French.

## DID YOU KNOW?

**Ecuador** means *Equator*: the Equator (0°) crosses the country
**Colombia** is named after Christopher Columbus, who sailed from Europe to the Americas in 1492
**Bolivia** is named after Simon Bolivar, a hero of the country's war of independence in the 1820s
**La Paz**, in Bolivia, means *peace*

***Cattle and cowboys.*** *To the south of the Amazon forest, there is a large area of dry woodland and grassland in Brazil called the Mato Grosso. Cattle are grazed here, and horses are still used to round them up.*

# TEMPERATE SOUTH AMERICA

### ARGENTINA

**AREA** 2,766,890 sq km
**POPULATION** 34,663,000
**MONEY** Peso

### CHILE

**AREA** 756,950 sq km
**POPULATION** 14,271,000
**MONEY** Peso

### URUGUAY

**AREA** 177,410 sq km
**POPULATION** 3,186,000
**MONEY** Peso

Chile is 4300 kilometres long, but it is only about 200 kilometres wide, because it is sandwiched between the Andes and the Pacific.

In the north is the Atacama Desert, the driest in the world. In one place, there was no rain for 400 years! Fortunately, rivers from the Andes permit some irrigation. Chilean nitrates come from this area. Nitrates are salts in dried-up lakes; they are used to make fertilizers and explosives. Copper is mined high in the mountains.

In the centre, the climate is like the Mediterranean area and California, with hot dry summers and warm wet winters with westerly winds. This is a lovely climate, and most Chileans live in this area.

In the south, Chile is wet, windy and cool. Thick forests which include the Chilean pine (monkey-puzzle tree) cover the steep hills. The reason for these contrasts is the wind. Winds bringing rain blow from the Pacific all year in the south; but only in winter in the centre; and not at all in the north.

**Geysers in the Andes, Chile.** *Hot steam hisses into the cold air, 4000 metres above sea level in the Andes of northern Chile. It shows there is still plenty of volcanic activity in the Andes.*

### PARAGUAY

**AREA** 406,750 sq km
**POPULATION** 4,979,000
**MONEY** Guarani

### STAMP

*Valparaiso is Chile's main port. It is on the coast near the capital. The city was founded in 1536 by the Spanish who arrived in the good ship Santiaguillo. Chile was ruled by the Spanish until 1818. Valparaiso means 'valley of paradise' – which is not quite true!*

## THE ANDES

The Andes are over 7000 kilometres long, so they are the longest mountain range in the world. They are fold mountains, with a very steep western side, and a gentler eastern side. Most of the high peaks are volcanoes: they are the highest volcanoes in the world. Mount Aconcagua (6960 metres) is extinct. Mount Guallatiri, in Chile, is the world's highest active volcano.

The higher you climb, the cooler it is. And the further you travel from the Equator, the cooler it is. Therefore, the snowline in southern Chile is much lower than in northern Chile.

**Sheep farming in Patagonia, Argentina.** *Southern Argentina has a cool, dry climate. Very few people live there – but lots of sheep roam the extensive grasslands. There are almost as many sheep in Argentina as there are people.*

**Argentina** means 'silvery' in Spanish: some of the early settlers came to mine silver. But today, Argentina's most important product is cattle. Cool grasslands called the Pampas (see map below) are ideal for cattle-grazing.

Argentina is a varied country: the north-west is hot and dry, and the south is cold and dry. The frontier with Chile runs high along the top of the Andes.

Buenos Aires, the capital city, is the biggest city in South America; it has 11 million people. The name means 'good air', but petrol fumes have now polluted the air.

**Paraguay** and **Uruguay** are two countries with small populations. Each country has under five million people. Nearly half the population of Uruguay lives in the capital city, Montevideo, which is on the coast. In contrast Paraguay is a landlocked country. Animal farming is the most important occupation in both these countries.

All these four countries – Chile, Argentina, Paraguay and Uruguay – have Spanish as their official language. Most of the people have European ancestors, except in Paraguay where there are a lot of South American Indians.

## THE FALKLAND ISLANDS

**Port Stanley,** capital of the Falklands, looks similar to an English town. These islands are a British colony in the South Atlantic. They are about 480 km east of Argentina, which claims them as the Islas Malvinas. Britain fought an Argentine invasion in 1982, and the military force is now as large as the population (only 2000). Sheep farming is the main occupation.

***Santiago, capital of Chile,*** has a beautiful setting between the Andes and the coastal mountains. A third of Chile's people live in Santiago. Its name means 'St James' – the patron saint of Spain, which once ruled Chile.

# THE ARCTIC

The Arctic is an ocean, which is frozen all through the winter and still has lots of ice in summer. It is surrounded by the northernmost areas of three continents, but Greenland is the only truly Arctic country.

For most of the year the land is snow-covered. During the short summer, when the sun never sets, the snow and the frozen topsoil melt. But the deeper soil is still frozen, so the land is very marshy. This treeless landscape is called the tundra.

The reindeer and caribou can be herded or hunted, but farming is impossible. In recent years, rich mineral deposits have been found. Canada, the USA and Russia have military bases near the Arctic Ocean.

From the Atlantic Ocean, there is easy access to the Arctic Ocean. But from the Pacific Ocean, the only route to the Arctic Ocean is the narrow Bering Strait, between Siberia (Russia) and Alaska (USA).

Fourth largest **ocean** – 14,090,000 sq km
**World record** for least sunshine
Surrounded by cold **land**
North Pole **first reached** in 1909

**The Inuit (Eskimo) village of Savissavik,** near Thule in northern Greenland. The houses are mostly wooden and are well insulated against the cold. They are built on stilts to protect them from the effects of frost moving the ground in winter, and to stop the warmth of the houses melting the ground beneath.

**Inuit (Eskimo)** fishing for cod through a crack in the spring ice. He has travelled over the sea from his village by sledge. Fish are a good source of protein for families in the far north.

## WILDLIFE IN GREENLAND

Land animals have to cope with very long winters. The Arctic fox turns white for camouflage.

KALAALLIT NUNAAT
400+50
GRØNLAND

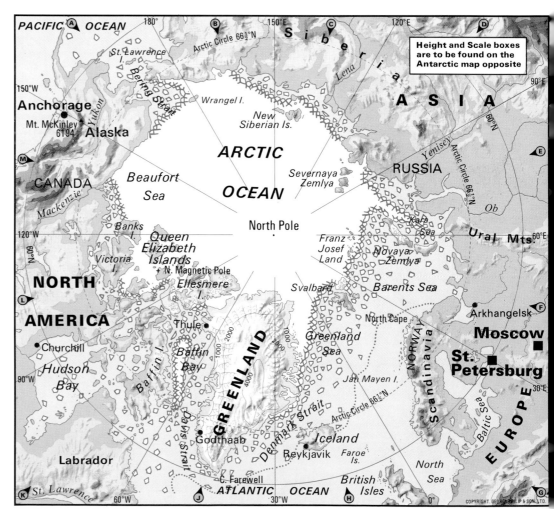

# ANTARCTICA

Antarctica is the continent surrounding the South Pole. It is the coldest, windiest and iciest place in the world! It is also very isolated, as the map shows.

No people live in Antarctica permanently. Some scientists work in research stations. Everything that is needed has to be brought in during the short summer. From November to January, icebreakers can reach the land. But huge icebergs are always a danger. In winter (May to July) it is always dark, the sea is frozen, and people have to face extreme cold and dangerous blizzards.

No-one 'owns' Antarctica. The Antarctic Treaty ensures that the continent should only be used for scientific research. This means it should remain peaceful for ever. The flags of the 32 nations that have signed the treaty stand in a ring round the South Pole, near the USA's Amundsen-Scott base. Even Antarctica has more and more tourists visiting the area every year.

Fifth largest **continent** – 14,100,000 sq km
**World record** for coldest temperature
Surrounded by cold **seas**
South Pole **first reached** in 1911

**Rookery of Gentoo Penguins in Antarctica.** *Penguins cannot fly, but they can swim very well. The parents use their feet to protect the eggs and chicks from the cold ice! No land animals live in Antarctica, but the ocean is full of fish, which provide food for penguins, seals and whales.*

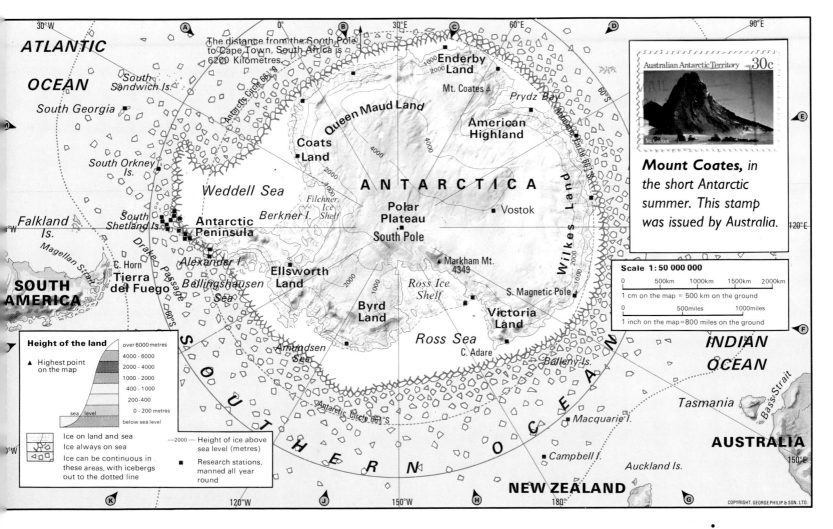

**Mount Coates,** *in the short Antarctic summer. This stamp was issued by Australia.*

Australian Antarctic Territory 30c

ATLANTIC OCEAN

South Sandwich Is.

South Georgia

The distance from the South Pole to Cape Town, South Africa is 6200 Kilometres.

Enderby Land

Mt. Coates ▲

Prydz Bay

South Orkney Is.

Queen Maud Land

American Highland

Coats Land

Weddell Sea

ANTARCTICA

A N T A R C T I C A

Filchner Ice Shelf

Polar Plateau

• Vostok

Berkner I.

Falkland Is.

South Shetland Is.

Antarctic Peninsula

South Pole

Wilkes Land

Magellan Strait

Drake Passage

C. Horn

Tierra del Fuego

Alexander I.

Bellingshausen Sea

Ellsworth Land

▲ Markham Mt. 4349

S. Magnetic Pole

SOUTH AMERICA

Byrd Land

Ross Ice Shelf

Victoria Land

Ross Sea

C. Adare

Amundsen Sea

INDIAN OCEAN

Balleny Is.

**Height of the land**

over 6000 metres
4000 - 6000
▲ Highest point on the map
2000 - 4000
1000 - 2000
400 - 1000
200 - 400
sea level
0 - 200 metres
below sea level

Ice on land and sea
Ice always on sea
Ice can be continuous in these areas, with icebergs out to the dotted line

—2000— Height of ice above sea level (metres)

■ Research stations, manned all year round

Tasmania

Bass Strait

AUSTRALIA

Macquarie I.

Antarctic Circle 66½°S

Campbell I.

Auckland Is.

SOUTHERN OCEAN

NEW ZEALAND

**Scale 1 : 50 000 000**

0   500km   1000km   1500km   2000km

1 cm on the map = 500 km on the ground

0   500miles   1000miles

1 inch on the map = 800 miles on the ground

COPYRIGHT. GEORGE PHILIP & SON. LTD.

**89**

# QUIZ QUESTIONS

## NAME THE COUNTRY

There is a long, thin country in almost every continent. Can you name the countries shown here – and name the continent in which they are found? (If you need help, look at pages 8–9 for a map of the countries of the world.)

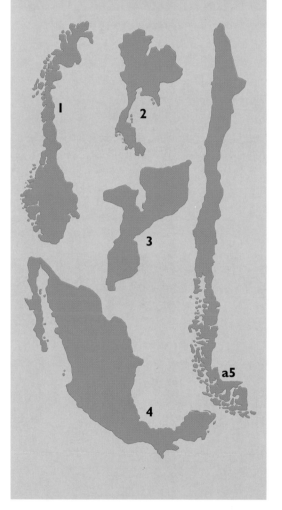

## NAME THE ISLAND

The name of the continent where each island is found is marked on each outline. Do you know (a) the name of each island, and (b) to which country each island belongs (or are they island countries)?

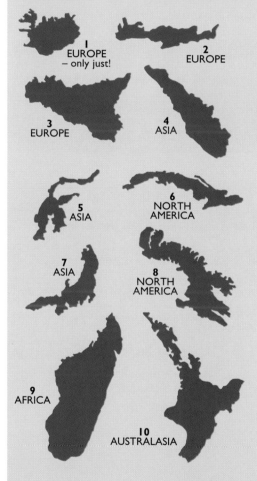

## GREAT RIVERS OF EUROPE

Use pages 18–37 to discover which great river flows through or near each pair of cities.
1  Vienna (Austria) and Budapest (Hungary)
2  Rotterdam (Netherlands) and Bonn (Germany)
3  Avignon (France) and Lyons (France)
4  Worcester (England) and Gloucester (England)
5  Toledo (Spain) and Lisbon (Portugal)

## A MYSTERY MESSAGE

Use the map of the countries of the world on pages 8–9 to decode this message. Each missing word is all or part of the name of a country. (For some answers, letters have to be taken out of or added to the name of the country.)

I was _ _ _ _ a _ _ (east of Austria), so I bought a large _ _ _ _ _ _ _ (east of Greece), some _ _ _ _ _ _ ns (east of Norway) and a bottle of _ _ _ _ ugal (west of Spain). Finally, I ate an _ _ _ land (west of Norway) -cream. I enjoyed my _ e _ _ i (east of Mauritania), but afterwards I began to _ _ _ _ earia (south of Romania) and I got a bad S _ _ _ _ (south of France). A O _ _ _ (east of Saudi Arabia) told me: 'Just eat Philip _ _ _ _ sapples (south of Taiwan) and _ _ gypt (east of Libya), cooked in a Ja _ _ _ (east of Korea). Tomorrow you can eat a Ghban _ _ _ (east of Ivory Coast) and some _ _ _ _ _ _ _ (east of Peru) nuts. It shouldn't _ _ _ _ _ a Rica (west of Panama) you too much.' I said: 'You must be _ _ _ agascar (east of Mozambique)! I think I've got _ _ _ _ ysr _ _ (north of Indonesia). I'll have _ _ / _ _ (west of Benin) to a doctor quickly, otherwise I'll soon be _ _ _ _ Sea (lake between Israel and Jordan).'
   Happily, the doctor _ _ bared (island country south of USA) me, so I am still M _ _ d _ _ _ s (islands west of Sri Lanka) today!

## PLACES IN ASIA

Move the letters to find:
*Countries*  RAIN; CHAIN; MOAN; AWAIT N; PLANE
*Capital cities*  ANIMAL; DIARY H; THE TANKS; A BULK; COOL MOB

## FIND THE COLOUR

Each answer is a colour. Use the atlas index and the maps to help you. Cover the right-hand column with a piece of paper and try to answer the left-hand column only. Award yourself 2 points for each correct answer to the left-hand column only, or 1 point if you used the clues in both columns.

1 A sea between Egypt and Saudi Arabia . . .

2 **A big island east of Canada . . .**

3 The sea between Turkey and Ukraine . . .

4 **The sea between Korea and China . . .**

5 The sea on which Arkhangelsk lies, in Russia . . .

6 **A town in southern France which is also a fruit . . .**

7 The tributary of the River Nile that flows from Ethiopia to Khartoum (Sudan) . . .

. . . and the river on the border of Oklahoma and Texas, USA.

**. . . and a bay on the west side of Lake Michigan, USA.**

. . . and a forest in Germany.

**. . . and a (stony) river in Wyoming, USA.**

. . . and the river flowing north from Lake Victoria to Khartoum (Sudan).

**. . . and the river which makes the border between South Africa and Namibia.**

. . . and a mountain ridge in eastern USA.

## OCEANS AND SEAS

What ocean would you cross on an aeroplane journey . . .

1 From Australia to the USA?
2 From Brazil to South Africa?
3 From Canada to Russia?
4 From Madagascar to Indonesia?
5 From Mexico to Portugal?

What sea would you cross on an aeroplane journey . . .

6 From Saudi Arabia to Egypt?
7 From Korea to Japan
8 From Denmark to the UK?
9 From Vietnam to the Philippines?
10 From Cuba to Colombia?

## THINGS TO DO

**COLLECT STAMPS WITH A THEME**
A stamp collection soon grows. Try a thematic collection: choose a theme (topic) and collect stamps on that theme. For example, you could collect:
*Flags on stamps* – such as the stamps of Estonia and Latvia on page 37.
*Map stamps* – small islands often issue map stamps to show everyone where they are!
*Traditional crafts* on stamps.

**COLLECT YOUR OWN COINS**
Ask people who have been abroad for any foreign coins they do not want – you will have an instant collection! If you cannot have the coins to keep, you could make pencil or crayon rubbings on thin paper. The coin box on page 16 is a good starting-point for making sense of the coins in your collection: each coin has a date, a value, a picture – and a country!

## USA STATES QUIZ

All the answers can be found on the maps on pages 62–3 and 66–9. Do not include Alaska and Hawaii.

1 Which is the *biggest* state?
2 Which is the *smallest* state?
3 Which state reaches furthest *north*? (Careful!)
4 Which state reaches furthest *south*?
5 Which state reaches furthest *west*?
6 Which state reaches furthest *east*?
7 Which state is split into two by a lake?
8 Which state is split into two by an inlet of the sea?
9 Which two states are perfect rectangles in shape?
10 Which state is shaped like a saucepan?
11 In which state will you be if you visit Lake Huron?
12 In which state will you be if you visit Lake Ontario?
13 In which state will you be if you visit the Great Salt Lake?
14 In which state will you be if you visit the Mississippi delta?
15 Which state in *northern* USA is called South . . . . . ?
16 Which state in *southern* USA is called North . . . . . ?
17 There is only one place in the USA where four states meet: which states?
18 How many states have a border with Mexico?
19 How many states have a coastline on the Pacific?
20 How many states have a coastline on the Gulf of Mexico?

## ANSWERS TO ALL QUIZ QUESTIONS ARE ON PAGE 96

# INDEX

## HOW TO USE THIS INDEX

The first number given after each name or topic is the page number; then a letter and another number tell you which square of the map you should look at.

For example, Abidjan is in square B2 on page 57. Find B at the top or the bottom of the map on page 57 and put a finger on it. Put another finger on the number 2 at the side of the map. Move your fingers in from the edge of the map and they will meet in square B2. Abidjan will now be easy to find. It is the capital city of the Ivory Coast, a country in West Africa.

If a name goes through more than one square, the square given in the index is the one in which the biggest part of the name falls.

Names like Gulf of Mexico and Cape Horn are in the Index as 'Mexico, Gulf of' and 'Horn, Cape'.

# INDEX

# ANSWERS TO QUESTIONS

**Page 6** 'RSA' stands for Republic of South Africa.

**Page 8** On this flag, the emblem of the United Nations is shown in white. This is the view of the world as it appears from above the North Pole. It is surrounded by olive branches of peace.

**Page 18** This building is in Brussels, Belgium: it was the headquarters of the European Union. Many important decisions were made here.

**Pages 18–19**
SF = Finland (Suomi Finland);
B = Belgium; L = Luxembourg;
DK = Denmark; F = France;
D = Germany (Deutschland in German); NL = Netherlands;
I = Italy; E = Spain (España);
S = Sweden; IRL = Ireland (Republic of Ireland);
A = Austria; GB = Great Britain;
P = Portugal; GR = Greece.

**Page 22** The London landmarks featured on the stamp are (*from left to right*): Westminster Abbey; Nelson's Column (in Trafalgar Square); statue of Eros (in Piccadilly Circus); Telecom Tower; clock tower of the Houses of Parliament (containing the bell Big Ben); St Paul's Cathedral; Tower Bridge; White Tower of the Tower of London.

**Page 24** Belgium has two official languages, Flemish and French. The coin on the right has the Flemish name for Belgium (*Belgie*); the coin on the left shows its French name (*Belgique*).

**Page 24** The yellow objects are CLOGS. They are shoes made out of wood. A few Dutch people still wear clogs, but tourists also like to buy them.

**Page 26** The photograph of the fruit stall shows: a watermelon, strawberries, blackberries, mangoes, pineapples, melons, cherries, avocados, tomatoes, apricots, peaches and nectarines.

**Pages 38–39** The script reads *across* the two pages:
1 Australia; 2 Egypt;
3 Hong Kong; 4 United States;
5 Taiwan.

**Page 39** The five countries which share the shoreline of the Caspian Sea are Russia, Kazakstan, Turkmenistan, Iran and Azerbaijan.

**Page 40** The 15 'new' countries formed at the break-up of the USSR are (*from largest to smallest*): Russia, Kazakstan, Ukraine, Turkmenistan, Uzbekistan, Belarus, Kyrgyzstan, Tajikistan, Azerbaijan, Georgia, Lithuania, Latvia, Estonia, Moldova and Armenia.

**Page 41** Moskva (= Moscow) to Vladivostok.

**Page 44** Clockwise (*from the top right-hand corner*), the picture shows: samosas, ground coriander, coriander leaves, cumin, pakoras, rice, poppadums, red chilli powder next to yellow turmeric powder, green okra (also called 'ladies' fingers'), garlic and bay leaves.

**Page 65** Australia, of course!

**Page 68** The north shores of Lakes Superior, Huron, Erie and Ontario are in Canada, and the south shores are in the USA. Lake Michigan is entirely in the USA.

**Page 69** El Salvador only has a coastline on the Pacific Ocean. Belize only has a coastline on the Caribbean Sea. (Honduras has a tiny coastline on the Pacific – look closely at the map!) One island has two countries on it: Haiti and Dominican Republic.

**Page 73** Seattle to Miami is 5445 kilometres; New Orleans to Chicago is 1488 kilometres.

**Page 76** The Spanish words mean:
Amarillo = Yellow;
Colorado = Coloured;
El Paso = The pass;
Los Angeles = The angels;
San José = St Joseph;
San Francisco = St Francis.

**Page 81** The islands of Guadeloupe and Martinique are both part of France. Curaçao is owned by the Netherlands; Turks Is, Caicos I. and Grand Cayman are owned by the UK. Some of the Virgin Islands belong to the UK, and some belong to the USA.

## ANSWERS TO QUIZ QUESTIONS (on pages 90–91)

### NAME THE COUNTRY
1 Norway (Europe)
2 Thailand (Asia)
3 Mozambique (Africa)
4 Mexico (Central America)
5 Chile (South America)

### NAME THE ISLAND
(Note: Name of country in brackets after name of island)
1 Iceland (Iceland)
2 Crete (Greece)
3 Sicily (Italy)
4 Sumatra (Indonesia)
5 Sulawesi (Indonesia)
6 Cuba (Cuba)
7 Honshu (Japan)
8 Baffin Island (Canada)
9 Madagascar (Madagascar)
10 North Island (New Zealand)

### A MYSTERY MESSAGE
I was *hungry*, so I bought a large *turkey*, some *swedes* and a bottle of *port*. Finally, I ate an *ice*-cream. I enjoyed my meal, but afterwards I began to *bulge* and I got a bad *pain*. A man told me: 'Just eat *pineapples* and *egg* cooked in a *pan*. Tomorrow you can eat a *banana* and some *Brazil* nuts. It shouldn't *cost* you too much.' I said: 'You must be *mad*! I think I've got *malaria*. I'll have *to* go to a doctor quickly, otherwise I'll soon be *dead*.'

Happily, the doctor *cured* me, so I am still *alive* today!

### GREAT RIVERS OF EUROPE
1 Danube; 2 Rhine;
3 Rhône; 4 Severn;
5 Tagus.

### PLACES IN ASIA
*Countries*
Iran; China; Oman; Taiwan; Nepal.
*Capital cities*
Manila; Riyadh; Tashkent; Kabul; Colombo.

### COLOUR QUIZ
1 Red (Red Sea/Red River)
2 Green (Greenland/Green Bay)
3 Black (Black Sea/Black Forest)
4 Yellow (Yellow Sea/ Yellowstone River)
5 White (White Sea/White Nile)
6 Orange (Orange/Orange River)
7 Blue (Blue Nile/Blue Ridge)

### STATES OF THE USA
1 Texas
2 Rhode Island
3 Minnesota
4 Florida
5 Washington
6 Maine
7 Michigan
8 Maryland
9 Wyoming and Colorado
10 Oklahoma
11 Michigan
12 New York
13 Utah
14 Louisiana
15 South Dakota
16 North Carolina
17 Utah, Colorado, Arizona and New Mexico
18 Four (California, Arizona, New Mexico and Texas)
19 Three (Washington, Oregon and California)
20 Five (Texas, Louisiana, Mississippi, Alabama and Florida)

### OCEANS AND SEAS
1 Pacific; 2 Atlantic;
3 Arctic; 4 Indian;
5 Atlantic; 6 Red Sea;
7 Sea of Japan; 8 North Sea;
9 South China Sea;
10 Caribbean Sea.

## PICTURE ACKNOWLEDGEMENTS

**Sue Atkinson** 66 bottom centre; **BBC Natural History Unit** /Keith Scholey 58 bottom left; **Colorsport** 22 centre right, /Bryan Yablonsky 72 top; **Finnish Tourist Board** 20 bottom centre; **Robert Harding Picture Library** 11 left, 11 right, 14, 20 top, 22 centre left, 28 centre right, 30 centre right, 30 bottom, 41 middle centre, 43 left, 44 top, 46 top, 48 centre left, 49 top left, 64 centre left, 64 centre right, 70 top, 70 bottom left, 70 bottom right, 79, 80 top, 80 bottom left, 81 left, 82, 86, 24 bottom centre, 34 bottom left, 36 centre right, 48 top right, 66 top left, 22 top, /David Beatty 40 bottom left, /Nigel Blythe 50 centre, /P. Bordes 56 top, /C. Bowman 32 centre, 78 top, /Rob Cousins 26 right, 46 bottom right, /Nigel Francis 26 centre left, 74 bottom, /Simon Harris 77 top, /Kim Hart 19 left, /Gavin Hellier 77 bottom, /Dave Jacobs 75 bottom, /F. Jackson 12 top, /Carol Jopp 15 right, /Thomas Laird 45 bottom, /Louise Murray 25, /Roy Rainford 23, 33, 74 top, /Geoff Renner 55, 87 top, 89, /Christopher Rennie 84 bottom right, /Michael Short 34 top right, /Adina Tovy 49 top right, /J. H. C. Wilson 45 top, /Nick Wood 66 bottom left, /Adam Woolfitt 19 centre; **James Hughes** 22 bottom right; **Hulton Deutsch Collection** 54 bottom left; **Hutchison Library** 24 centre, 40 centre bottom, 68, /Sarah Errington 58 top, 85, /Bernard Gerard 20 bottom right, /Tony Souter 30 centre left, 32; **Image Bank** 24 top, /Walter Bibikow 22 bottom left, /Gallant 42 top, /L. D. Gordon 87 bottom, /Bullaty Lomeo 36 top right, /Michael Melford 32 top, /Kaz Mori 75 top, /Jeffrey M. Spielman 8, /Harald Sund 40 top right, /Hans Wolf 28 top right, 28 bottom left; **Nina Jenkins** 54 centre, 56 centre right; **Japan National Tourist Organization** 50 top left; **Steve Nevill** 76 bottom; **Panos Pictures** /Gary John Norman 57 left; **Planet Earth Pictures** 60 top, /G. Cafiero 43 right, /John Eastcott 76 centre, 6, 88 below, /John Lythgoe 54 bottom right, 78 centre right, /John Waters/Bernadette Spiegel 39 top; **Reed International Books Ltd** /James Johnson 26 bottom, /Graham Kirk 78 bottom left, /NASA 4, /Paul Williams 46 bottom centre; **Russia & Republics Photolibrary** /Mark Wadlow 40 bottom right, 41 top; **South American Pictures** /Tony Morrison 83; **Still Pictures** /B. & C. Alexander 88 top, /Chris Caldicott 53, 54 top, /Mark Edwards 56 bottom left, 84 bottom left, /Michel Gunther 58 bottom centre, /John Maier 10 top, 61, /Roland Seitre 62; **Tony Stone Images** 28 bottom centre, 50 top right, 66 bottom right, /Doug Armand 67 top, /John Beatty 86 bottom, /Stephen Beer 60 bottom left, /Richard Bradbury 69, /Suzanne & Nick Geary 64 centre, 76 top, /Walter Geiersberger 29, /George Grigoriou 34 bottom right, 35 top, /Gavin Hellier bottom left, /Simone Huber 19 right, /Dave Jacobs 72 bottom, /H. Richardson 71, /Hideo Kurihara 64 top, /Alain le Garsmeur 48 bottom right, bottom centre, /John Noble 84 bottom centre, /Nicholas Parfitt 59, /Greg Pease 74 centre, /Pete Seaward 30 top, /Simpson 84 top, /Zygmunt Nowak Solins 37 centre top, /Nabeel Turner 42 bottom right, 50 bottom, /Art Wolfe 65, /Trevor Wood 44 left; **Judy Todd** 38 top right; **David & Jill Wright** bottom, 15 left, 16, 18, 20 bottom left, 21, 24 bottom right, 26 top left, 26 top right, 37 bottom right, 42 bottom left, 44 centre, 46 bottom left, 52 bottom, 57 right, 58 bottom right, 60 bottom centre, 67 bottom, 81 right.